DAMAGED GOODS

A woman who became her own hero

G L E N N A   M C C A R T H Y

ISBN: 9781520363509

Contents

INTRODUCTION   1

1. EMERGENCY CONTACT (2012)   3
2. JUST AN ILLUSION (1994)   9
3. WAR STORIES (2012)   15
4. IT CAN'T GET BETTER THAN THIS (2009)   21
5. ST. PATRICK'S DAY   37
6. BUILDING 101   43
7. PICKING UP THE PIECES (2012)   57
8. BLACKOUT (1999)   65
9. TOUGH GUY (2002)   75
10. AIDS AND CONFUSED (1990)   83
11. FRENCHY (1998)   93
12. WHAT NAME ARE YOU USING? (1985)   99
13. HEALTHY GOODBYES (2015)   105
14. S.H.U (2001)   113
15. FIRST ATTEMPT, 2004   121
16. PLEASANTVILLE   129
17. IDENTITY CRISIS (2014)   133
18. BING MONSTER (1999)   141
19. GROWING PAINS (2016)   153
20. SOLITUDE   161
21. PAINFUL REALIZATIONS   169
22. GROUND ZERO (2016)   179

FINAL THOUGHTS   185
AFTER THE TURNAROUND   189

Acknowledgements

There are several people who've touched my life. They include Charlene Griffin, Steve Carras, Steve Johnson, Peter Panken, Nedra Lewis, Beth Sears, Danielle Brummer, David and Jimmy Higa from CVTC, Debra Greenwood, Mrs. Lockwood, Rachel Falkenstern, Erica Sepalla, Hilary McGovern, Mrs. Farah from Beacon Mayra Herrera and my 'Carty Clan' nephews. I would also like to thank Joe Turner from 'Exponents' for investing in me.

Not to forget, a woman who has been there for as long as I can remember. She has been selfless and has supported my family in different ways. She is the beautiful hearted Sharon Gregg. Two organizations that have been instrumental in my getting an education are the College Community Fellowship and The College Initiative – both have been lifesavers.

Back on My Feet is a great organization that reaches out to the underserved. They help people refocus their energy by running as well as exercising.

I am a terrible listener and listening to Eckhart Tolle on an audiobook was exactly what the doctor ordered. His wisdom and clarity was calming and helped me center myself. I have read and listened to over a dozen of his works.

I would like to thank the TV show Pit Bulls and Parolees because they are my kind of people. On this list is another TV show Impractical Jokers, because it works very well in replacing the endorphin rush of drugs. Laughter, in a way, is my new drug. Both shows helped me get through a rough time.

Last, but far from least, is the man who got me started on my journey of self-repair, Ken Siegel. His timing was vital in saving my life. Later, I went on to meet his wife Dorothy, who touched my life as well.

I would also like to thank my demons for riding me so hard, I had no choice but to stop, slow down and face the change. Sure as hell, it's been one crazy ride. I hope this memoir wakes a lot of people up and shows them anything is possible.

Oh, and consider this. How many addicts does it take to change a light bulb? The answer is zero. We're so afraid of change we'd rather remain in the dark.

Introduction

After you're done reading Glenna's story, you cannot help but admit she's led a hard life. She's gone through more than her fair share of trouble, in different ways. Some of it she invited; some she did not. To say that she had a troubled childhood would be an understatement.

Cutting a long story short, she spent a considerable time working as a prostitute. She was a drug addict. Somewhere along the way, she caught AIDS and Hepatitis C. She successfully battled the latter, which she considers a battle won.

A turnaround in such scenarios is rare. Glenna, though, felt it was imminent. Along the way, she met some good people. She managed to get the better of her paranoia and anxiety, successfully completing her bachelor's degree in sociology. Now, she's happy how things have shaped up. She knows the journey is nowhere near the end, and understands she'll have to deal with new kinds of challenges, but they're ones she looks forward to, unlike before.

1.
Emergency Contact (2012)

"Do you want to use the same emergency contact?" the nurse asked. "Huh," I replied, in a daze. "Do you want me to use the same emergency contact?" she repeated. "What? Let me see." I looked at the paper and saw the name of my ex-boyfriend. I almost laughed at myself for using him as a contact. "Umm, well, can you leave it blank?"

I was trying to convince myself it didn't bother me – that I could not give a person's name with any confidence. I shifted focus. The situation seemed almost unreal because I had wished this on someone, the same someone listed as my emergency contact. No, I am not into voodoo or witchcraft.

This once, someone yelled to me on a crowded prison bus, asking me how my 'man' was. This was when we were travelling from one facility to another. Since I liked playing to the crowd, I had specifically said, "Oh, fuck that scrub. I hope he's got every STD we ain't already got." As we laughed, I also blurted out, "I hope that bitch gets scabies and rabies." At the time, I didn't even know what scabies meant. I was simply trying to be a wise ass.

Then, there I was, approximately two years later, although I still felt like the 'good guy'. Words from my previous relationship had came back to haunt me. I had caught scabies in prison, after which I was treated like a leper. On that fateful day, a dog bit me, and I was getting rabies shots in my head, due to it being the wound area.

"Hey! I'm hungry. Can I go back to the waiting area and get some food from the vending machine?" I asked. The nurse didn't answer, which I considered a yes. I wasn't even hungry. For some reason, I felt compelled to show people the dried up blood all over my head and body. Don't get me wrong, I didn't want anybody's sympathy. Fuck that.

I hoped to become relevant to somebody, even if it was just out of shock value or being nosey. I was sure the emergency room had seen more graphic emergencies, a lot worse. That notwithstanding, I continued to parade myself back and forth to the waiting area, just to see people's heads turn. I had my poker face because I did not want anyone to think I was the weak victim sort. I wore my battle scars proudly.

A dog at the shelter where I volunteered had attacked me. I

still love the dogs, though. As crazy as it might sound, I relate to a stray dog in a cage that is turned vicious by people, because only then does it becomes an outcast. If one dog decided he wanted to hurt me, it didn't take away from the hundreds that made me smile and taught me how to 'feel' again.

On that day, I had been practicing my tough guy role. Despite warning, I took a large 127-pound dog into the backyard at the shelter. I had already been told some people were scared to deal with him. I figured he would know I was on his side. Once exhausted, I let him of the leash and sat on the ground, Indian style, listening to music on my iPod. I was watching him run around, thinking I was giving him a break from the confinement that animals have to endure at shelters.

He came up and was not even growling. He mounted my folded legs and looked over my head. I thought he was sniffing my ear so I went to hug him. Like lightning, I felt the force, and then the teeth sunk into my head. I rolled on my stomach so he couldn't get my face. I played dead because I knew didn't have a chance otherwise.

It worked. When he did not get a reaction, I guess he felt that he had shown dominance. He walked away. There was one more volunteer assigned in the caged area. Without hesitation, she came out to help. I jumped up and tried to push her into a safe zone, in case the dog was still aggressive.

She loved dogs as much as me and started making excuses for his behavior, saying he was scared. I found out later that the dog had taken half a woman's face off. I also met the person who brought the dog to the shelter.

My head was bleeding profusely. I walked back into the

main building and had the veterinarians call an ambulance. We couldn't figure out which part of my head was bleeding because there was too much blood. At one point, I yelled at them, "don't touch the blood, get bleach," because I knew I had HIV and Hepatitis C. I was at a point in my life where I was not ashamed to warn people and educate them on the subject. It had been over 20 years since I was diagnosed positive.

The ambulance driver asked if I had any health issues. As usual, I resorted to humor to answer a difficult question. I laughingly said, "You got a lot of time. Yeah. I got HIV and Hepatitis C, but don't worry." I told him to be careful, given the possibility of coming in contact with HIV.

"Actually I am more concerned about Hepatitis C," he responded. "Why?" I asked. "It is more dangerous due to the fact that it can survive in oxygen a lot longer than HIV," he answered. "I thought you can only get Hepatitis C from needles." I said. "No, you can get it from sex and contact with contaminated blood," he added.

I felt a little embarrassed because I was an HIV/AIDS speaker and peer educator in prison. When women told me they had Hepatitis C but never used a needle, I thought they were full of shit. I sat in the ambulance, looking back at when I was a speaker, and how I dealt with the responsibility. I had to confess to myself that I was not doing it only to help others. I was also using it as a venting tool and a way to be the center of attention.

I kept talking about diseases and my past with the ambulance workers. When I got to the emergency room, I was left alone with a towel wrapped around my head. It was time to take a stroll to the vending machine.

Suddenly, a doctor came in and examined my head, while I was busy chatting away. He told me to "be quiet," because I got bit in a main artery. Me not shutting up kept blood squirting out of the wound, requiring the doctor to use staples. I tried very hard to shut up and stop cracking jokes and breathe, which was not one of my strong points.

He went to get the rabies shots for my head due to my immune-deficiency disorder. He was going directly in the wound area. I had endured the staples and was waiting for the injections. Only, I didn't know what was coming. That rabies shots hurt a lot is not a myth, I found out that day.

While waiting, for what seemed like a very long time, I caught sight of a social worker I dealt with from 'The Coming Home Program." It was a support group for felons in Saint Luke's Hospital. "Hey Brenda, what are you doing here?" I asked. She came over and looked at me kind of puzzled, asking what happened. After exchanging reasons, she asked, "Who is coming to pick you up?"

Again, someone asked me a question that kicked up feelings. "Oh, I am okay, and I am used to emergency rooms," I joked. She asked why nobody was there with me. I told her I didn't want to bother people with something I could handle by myself. In reality, I felt very alone, as I had my entire life.

The icing on the cake was her asking, "Glenna, do you have any friends?" I did not answer for a moment. While I knew a whole lot of people, I didn't even remember half of them. Where I was that night, after quickly evaluating my social circle, my answer was a straightforward "No."

2.
Just an Illusion (1994)

I woke up and the first thing I saw was the underside of an overpass. I was laying on tracks located on the West Side of Midtown Manhattan in New York City. I suddenly realized I was naked and had been stripped of everything – from socks and underwear, to jewelry and ID. Someone had overpowered and violated me, leaving me unconscious.

I got up to assess my situation and figure out what I was going to do next. Strangely, I was not concerned about my orifices or possible damage to my body in any kind of way. At that point, my priority was to find my Benefit Card, because I was getting money the next day. I was definitely not going to let someone take away my day of being able to self-medicate without having to perform sex for money.

I stood up. Since it was dark I assumed it was obviously an hour in the night. I realized I must have been unconscious (or sleeping) for hours, because the episode took place around midday.

Well, no sense figuring out the entire silly details because it is done now. I was alive, so I had more important things to do such as find my Welfare Card.

Back then; I was a 'garbage head'. It simply meant I   used

many and any type of mood-altering substances, including legal ones that were helpful because they let me get high for free. They worked as backup drugs, given that I had to be sedated at all times.

I was on a very high dosage of Methadone and was also prescribed Xanax. My psychiatrist was so cool; he gave me a script of 8mg a day. I might have been overmedicated, but that was the point, right? Being high and feeling nothing.

I had to find my card because I was going to be sick from withdrawal soon. I would rather not have woken up than to feel that. Benzodiazepines such as Xanax affect your memory, which was unknown to me at the time. Besides, I honestly did not care about what the long-term risks were. My main objective was to beat the clock in trying to run away from feeling anything; I just wanted to be comfortably numb.

The way the situation came about was very simple, I was unhappy and lonely; I needed to try and find a comfort zone. It was not irregular for me to actually sell myself to buy a paid audience. I believed there was no unconditional love or true friendships. I sensed it was all about manipulation and ego.

I hated being a prostitute because it felt like an out of body experience. After all, you have to shut down and go through the motions. As a result, when I found a way to be safe in my skin, with no obligations or conditions, shutting down became a norm.

In order to have control, I had to bring something to the table. I thought it was the only way people would be nice to me. I was used to a world where everything was conditional. Just like I was used, I figured I could return the favor, and we could use each other, so to speak. You pretended you were interested   in my rambling on, life, and stories and you laughed at my jokes. In turn, I would supply the drugs.

I definitely did not want sex; I just wanted an illusion of companionship and bonding with someone. When the drugs ran out, I got anxious, because I knew I had an expensive heroin habit. I also got anxious because I was losing my leverage as far as company.

It is a crazy life with a vicious cycle, that of an addict. Sometimes you have to make your own realities. Kicking dope and pills is not a nice reality trust me.

Earlier that day I managed to make some money in Midtown. When it came time to buy my non-prescribed drugs, I realized I had extra money, which was unusual. I figured I could ask someone to get high with me – not a hard task, especially when it's not at his or her cost.

I finally found a guy who looked like he might be a male hustler (man on man prostitute), and figured it was the safest way to go. I also figured if I dealt with people who had their own demons, they would never judge me. Oh, and just because they hustle men does not necessarily mean they are gay; it often serves as a means to an end. For instance, I was a prostitute but did not enjoy sex for a long time, not even with my relationships.

We engaged in some small talk and I asked, "Do you want to get high?" The rest, as the saying goes, is history. We went to the tracks on the West Side of Midtown Manhattan because they were isolated and underground while also being accessible and visible in some areas.

We laughed as we went through the broken fence, and scurried down the hill to the tracks. We were acting like kids who were cutting school and were amused with pushing boundaries. Breaking rules was a thrill, almost like it was an achievement in life.

It was a fair deal to me – I give you crack and you pretend to be my friend – so it started off on a good note. We laughed and talked.

Suddenly, though, the mood changed, and his demeanor became totally different. "So, what up?" he said. "With what?" I asked. He pointed to his crotch and said, "You know what time it is." "Are you for real?" I retorted, "this is MY CRACK so why the fuck would I suck your dick?"

I was getting nervous and angry at the same time, because the illusion was over and this reality was not part of the plan. I continued to try and tell him he must be fucking crazy if he thought I just came back from sucking dick, that I was on my time and who the fuck did he think he was. He said, "You got a big mouth bitch; I will make you...

I don't know who threw the first punch, but we started fighting. I guess I was out of my league because I must have got knocked out. One terrible thing about being on massive drugs is you can't even count on your own memory after the fact. It is usually sketchy and scattered.

There I was, stripped completely naked. I was having a panic attack because funds for my next fix were gone and my new friend plan backfired. I walked around on the tracks. Even though it was dark, the moon was out overhead. I walked on the track because I was on an exposed part. I saw a garbage can on fire in the distance, about a block away. There were some people around it, probably homeless men.

I looked under every dirty newspaper and rummaged through garbage. To my dismay, I did not find my card. I finally realized I had to get home and had no clothes. It is amazing how fast you can think when you have to.

I saw an umbrella that had been tossed down from the overpass, I guess due to being broken. It was a large black standard umbrella. I started pulling the fabric off the frame and finally ended up with something that looked like a tablecloth with metal attachments. I wrapped it around myself and climbed up the same dirty hill that I had climbed down earlier, but I wasn't laughing.

I lived with a friend on 49th Street and 10th Avenue, so it was going to be a 2-avenue/4-block sprint. I was glad it was very late and the traffic was minimal. I ran with this umbrella wrapped around me like a mini dress, with the crack of my ass hanging out. I actually made it home without incident.

When I got to my building and rang the bell, my roommate answered and asked, "Where are your keys?" "Just let me in," I said in distress. Upon opening the door he asked, "What the hell are you wearing?" "Long story, hey, can I borrow some money?" was my reply.

3.
War Stories (2012)

"Yo, I am tired of hearing your fucking war stories!" a woman blurted out, from the other side of the room. This was in my psychology class on a Friday night. Was she talking to me, I thought to myself. It became obvious she was, and I tried to play it smooth.

"Huh, I wasn't telling war stories – I was talking about DMX and the how the music you listen to gives some insight into your mindset," I said in my defense. "I don't give a fuck about DMX either," she replied.

Damn, I had all eyes on me and the tension in the room was palpable. So much so, you could hear a pin drop. However, I could not fight, it was college. Besides, I was on probation. I felt that familiar fight-or-flight feeling going into overdrive, but I could not look like a punk. Who was this woman anyway?

I tried to turn around to my left and see who she was, but my shoulder and neck problem impeded proper movement. In reality, the other side of the room was very irrelevant. They were the wallflowers, on their phones, never adding anything to the conversations. I assumed that was the way they liked it. Obviously, I was wrong.

I was in college, so why did I feel like I was about to get into a fight? In psychology class? Was this for real? It was a three-hour Friday night class and the professor had a free-spirited curriculum, meaning we could talk about life and experiences. That was my cue. Even though I had a bad cold and was drinking green tea, I still could not shut up. The show had to go on and I didn't know how to relax without a distraction such as talking.

A few months ago, I walked into this class and sat right in the front, near the teacher's desk. As the night passed, I was surrounded by a bunch of young women who were very attractive. Not that I cared, but women do check out their competition. The one to my right had a butt that would make JLo envious. The woman who sat on the other side was, I later found out, a Nigerian beauty pageant winner. Let me not forget the two blondes behind me.

The entire class had been sub-divided into study groups based on where one was sitting. To my surprise, I actually liked the women in my group. Usually, I don't like being around women, but we bonded. It was a good experience for me to see that not all women argue and talk shit to each other, and can actually get along. Well, at least up until that night.

I had felt awkward going back to school. However, since I got fired from a volunteer job working with animals for being a liability, my friend talked me into it. I registered for school figuring they were never going to take me back, given that I had been to prison twice. To my surprise, I got back in without incident, based on a technical mistake.

I was broke and didn't have the latest laptop, which led to same inferior feeling I had as a child in a private school on a scholarship. My mantra back then was, when in doubt, over-compensate with bravado. I was twice everyone's age, so I did my usual and over compensated with my street knowledge.

I had to bring something to the table, or so I thought. Just my luck! A stranger with a big mouth was going to make me prove myself. It seems like no matter how far you get from street life, there is always something that wants to help you self-sabotage.

Well, show time! I hated women in general, because I never had a positive experience growing up with them. I had no daughters or sisters and every parental female had been a control freak. From the Ivy League to the ghetto woman, women were not a source of happiness.

I tried to reason with her saying we could talk after class, and we didn't have to put on a show. She, however, kept going on and on. Finally, I said, "Whatever, bitch!" Next, I heard chairs flying, and this young woman that looked Hispanic was coming at me like a freight train. I was surprised because I have had more fights in my life than I can remember, and I had never seen someone this angry. It was like we had been enemies for a lifetime.

I got up to get into a fighting stance. To my amazement, my 'study group' friends also stood up, making a wall between us. I have never had anyone protect me like that. They didn't hit her, but they made it clear that they did not want me to fight or get hurt.

At this point, the teacher grabbed her arm and started pulling her out of class. She was still ranting and raving. Although I was happy that my newfound friends had spared me a fight, there was more to it than that. I would have fought like my life depended on it and both of us would have been kicked out of school; me for sure, given my history. My new friends saved my life because they saved my future.

I was stuck and touched, yet my pride had to get the last word. She was telling me to "Take it outside," inviting me to the fight out of the room. I took a sip of my green tea and said, "Get your fat ass out of here and shut the fuck up!"

Again, I set off a bomb. She freed herself from the professor and started charging towards me once more. I instinctively threw my green tea at her, over the heads of the people in the way. She slipped, and so did the professor, who was still trying to contain the situation. They were actually wrestling on the floor. Finally, he got her to stand up and walked her out. Then came security, and we had to fill out incident reports.

It felt like a dream. I was nervous that the tea throwing would get me in trouble. What followed was security ending the class for the night. After laughing, talking, and revisiting what happened, we were ready to leave, standing by the elevator. When the door to the elevator opened we saw the angry Hispanic woman in it – she was being escorted by security. We just stared at her and, as the door closed, she stared back.

I had a weird déjà vu kind of experience then, because that was usually my role. The loner that acts out and is thrown out – where I leave alone. We took the stairs and went across the street, to Chicatellis, to grab a bite. We joked and I said, "Don't fuck with me or I will throw some green tea on your ass." At the same time, while it looked like the Hispanic, who was a force to be reckoned with, wanted to kill me, I still felt bad.

When you throw your life away so many times and have been by yourself to figure it out, it is a very hard way to go later. One day, I heard her talk, sharing something she witnessed in her family. Being self-absorbed, it slipped my mind.

I know what it feels like to be overwhelmed and hate the world. How can I hate someone when I know what pain feels like?

4.
It Can't get Better Than This (2009)

"Yo miss, I don't want to see the crack of your ass all in my face," I heard someone say from behind me. This was while I stumbled, trying to balance myself on one leg, taking my pants off to shower. Maybe I should've undressed in the shower area. I felt like a nervous zombie who was running on fumes and faking norms from memory, trying to pretend I was still alive.

Mind you, this was the belly of the beast (Rikers Island Jail). While all the inmates looked like they were smoking dynamite, everyone was real quick to talk about others. There, this woman was complaining about my ass being "all in her face," even though she was over 25 feet away! I tried to ignore her.

"Yo, I know you heard me!" she shouted. Sometimes, the barbarian effect is right on point with people like these. Only, she was in a wheelchair and I wouldn't get any points if I reacted and beat her ass. If I lost, well, my ego just couldn't take that chance. I decided to let it slide. Don't step on these 'wheelchair gangsters' because they are the first ones to forget they are disabled.

You would think the hostility between inmates would be at a low in an infirmary, since everyone is sick in some kind of way. The scenario was far from it in this joint. In the infirmary, women got into more fights and arguments than inmates in general population.

I used the passive aggressive approach saying, "Yo, I am not the arguing type," implying, I don't argue, I fight. Unfortunately, it backfired and she started barking, "Yo, you wanna fight?" Once again, I got a maniac in a wheelchair. This was not the first time.

I had a fight with a wheelchair gangster about a decade ago, in the same building. This time, however, I chose to walk into the shower area to defuse the situation, pretending she wasn't that important.

In all honesty, I take confrontation very seriously and anticipate the worst. I suffer from paranoia and anxiety, I guess because of going through opiate withdrawal. As a result, I think about confrontation obsessively, planning and plotting to the point where my stomach does back flips waiting for my cue. In most cases, it doesn't amount to shit, with all that energy wasted for nothing.

I hoped the hot water was working. It was the only perk of getting up when the body felt like every nerve ending was screaming. My legs were jelly. I felt cold, then hot. My hands were shaking badly. This is the price you pay for being numb on the street with drugs. Eventually, life catches up and hits you like a power punch in your soul.

I ran the water to see if the temperature was good. In reality, nothing felt good. I knew I was in for the ride of my life because I kicked my methadone and Xanax habit. I knew from experience this was hell on earth.

At Rikers Island, everyone studies everyone. Even if you feel like death, sometimes it is better to front like you are on point and ready for action, just to avoid bullshit. People analyze everything you do, from how you talk on the phone, to what you buy at commissary, to how much you spend and even how many times you brush your teeth. Your everyday actions get clocked, to be used as potential ammunition later.

I can't even begin to tell you what a culture shock it is to see life without drugs, going through withdrawal in that environment. You have to keep on going because you do not have a choice. Death would be a welcome alternative in comparison to withdrawal symptoms.

Finally, after the lights went off and nobody was yelling, fighting or blasting the TV, I lay on bed thinking the whole situation was like a movie. This could not be my life.

The next day I woke up and heard someone yelling, "Medication," which included methadone. Everyone scrambles to be first in line for their methadone, or whatever meds they are taking. There is a 'me first' psychosis in jail, which can give me an anxiety attack. While I try to avoid crowded areas I don't have that luxury all the time. Sometimes, I wait for the smoke to clear and then get up.

Someone else yelled, "Yeah, go get your jungle juice," to which a few people snickered. This is a classic example of 'birds of a feather' as they are not 'dope fiends'. Some people like to crack jokes because they are not going through withdrawal, and dope fiends put down 'crack heads'. I was a self-proclaimed garbage head, given that I did all drugs besides marijuana. Weed made me nervous. However, my drug of choice was heroin.

The woman who slept in the bed next to mine had gotten real friendly with me. I knew how the game went, so I took it for what it was worth, which was not much – I just played the game until the truth revealed itself.

One day she said to me, "Watch my back, I am going to take that woman's shit." I was like, huh? She got up, walked over to another woman's bed, and picked two pairs of reading glasses. I couldn't believe she was serious and how conspicuous the act was. She came back and hid them. I asked her, "Why did you do that?" When she told me how much they were worth, I wondered what kind of people could identify valuable stuff lying around in such a place. Thieves, was my guess.

I thought the incident was unnecessary and cold. The woman she stole from was old, and after the theft, probably couldn't read anything.

There's a saying on the street and in jail – mind your business – I never liked being part of it. Personally, I don't like thieves; I shouldn't say I don't like them because I don't really know them. After all, I don't get close to anyone to care enough. What I do know, though, is thieves are sneaky, and not to be trusted.

During the 80's, with all the chain-snatching and people getting robbed, I never got jewelry ripped off my neck or ears. It was surprising because it was mandatory to wear gold, and lots of it. When people like me who were broke made sure we looked like Christmas trees it was funny, because none of us even had a bank account.

Sadly, my associates, people I thought I could trust, did rob me on a few occasions. I was always shocked when an associate turned out to be a con artist by trade, and was dishonest with me. How dare they? They never took anything by force; they typically got me on a sneak tip, like when I was sleeping or high. I once woke up with my sneaker slit from heel to toe because that's where I put my money. That thieving bastard performed surgery on my sneaker while I slept like I was overdosed. I was probably close to overdosing anyway.

There is a hierarchy in jail and it's just like life in the free (read capitalist) world. Thieves put down hoes, and hoes put down each other depending on whether they are with pimps or if they are 'renegades', which is what I was. A renegade operates independently, which might sound cool, but it's not. The downside with street hoes who are renegades is they have pimps called 'drugs'. There is no independence in reality.

A few thieves who were also hoes told me I was a 'flat-backer', which means a prostitute that actually has sex. They boasted of just keeping their legs tight, with a penis never having penetrated them. Yeah, right! They lured guys for sex, snatched their wallets when they were not looking, and sent them on their way, none the wiser, so they said. That was surely not the case with me.

Again, my ego does not go down easily. I was an honest prostitute; I got paid for services and did what was agreed on. That made me an honorable righteous prostitute, right? Then again, I had AIDS. In my defense, I didn't give it to anyone because I always used a condom. I had to do what I had to do to earn money, right?

I can do the comparing game and find faults in my peers to the point where I feel superior. In reality, I haven't felt good about my existence for as long as I can remember. I wasn't supposed to live this long, which is why I never thought I would have to carry this baggage for so long.

The life of an addict, as I've said before, and probably will again, is a vicious cycle. I could not deal with my life, so I needed to self-medicate. To do that, you need money. You do things that make you feel hollow and soulless, thinking you can be numb again soon, and forget what you did. Wake up and do it all over the next day. Drug addiction, vicious!

The coast looked clear. I got up and went to the medication window where they gave me my methadone. The dosage was being reduced since as I had a felony. They didn't give me anything for my benzo withdrawal and I really needed it. I said to the woman, "I need the other stuff, you know, for the pills." I couldn't even think right or remember the name. All I knew was I needed it badly. The response I got was, "You are done with that, you are only getting methadone now."

I felt my heart drop because it was the beginning of the hardest part of going to jail – being sick mentally and physically, with amplified reactions due to withdrawal. I already felt bad with the meds, and without warning they deemed me fit not to die from kicking more than one drug. That was the reason I was in the infirmary. Rikers doesn't care if your life is miserable, but they don't want you dying on their shift. If you're addicted to more than one extreme drug, they will put you in the infirmary to cover their asses.

An argument broke out across the room with someone yelling, "Yo, it's too early for all that noise!" The next thing, there was an argument with one woman saying, "Don't let these diapers fool you – I will bust your ass!" Incoherent verbal exchanges followed as I stood there thinking I didn't know she was wearing diapers. I guess everyone knows now!

The girl in question was young and people said she has AIDS, which unfortunately is not a shocker in jail. There was also a rumor that she had thrush, a contagious bacterial infection in the mouth. She was always quick to try and get a drag of your cigarette, although we were not supposed to be smoking in the infirmary. As far as I was concerned, we all lived in glass houses. I didn't care what you had, as long as you didn't mess with me.

Sometimes fighting can be relaxing simply because it gives you a release. However, when the storm hits and passes, you realize it wasn't even worth it in the first place. Egos are in overdrive in confined spaces, with everyone trying to prove themselves. People who feel angry, inferior and neglected act out in irrational ways, when all they have is a sense of pride, as false as it may be.

Personally, I don't like to give up on my ego. When I have problems with people, I try not to fight. I understand now, that sometimes it is unavoidable, at least in my mind. Back then, at its worst, my ego was full of hate and criticism. I was walking around trying to figure out who needed to get their ass kicked.

On occasions, my neighbor who stole was put in the quarantine room. It was in the infirmary, with a visible window. While she wasn't a biohazard, she caused problems repeatedly. When they tried to put her back in general population, she kept reminding them she was pregnant. I guess the initial health reasons for putting her there took precedence at such times. The authorities simply isolated her from everybody as and when needed.

I got a new neighbor who was white. She said she "did not belong in places like this." I kind of laughed to myself thinking how many serial killers felt the same way. I felt she better learn to fight quickly or at least create an impression that she was up for it. After all, she had money was going to become very popular soon. She would learn about 'friends' in jail. The weaker people are the easiest to spot.

"McCarthy!" I heard my name yelled out, and I asked my new neighbor "Did they just call my name?" It was funny because how would she know? While you're just a number in jail and called by your last name, I'm sure my name was the last thing on her mind. I got up and approached the 'bubble', which is the officers' station, and asked, "Did you call me?"

"What's your name?" "Glenna McCarthy," I replied. "Yes, pack your shit because you're moving," she said. "Moving where?" I asked. "You don't have to worry about that right now, just get your shit together because the escort is on her way," she added.

Hell no! I thought, with my legs jiggling and my body feeling like a football team jumped me. I was going to general population, which was a whole different ball game. You don't know if you're going to a dorm or a building with cells. Personally, I prefer being in a cell because I can sleep better knowing I'm sharing it only with my own demons, and not other people's. Not to forget, you get your own toilet, which is a luxury in jail.

"I am still on methadone," I pleaded "still detoxing." "Well that's above my pay grade," she blurted, and dismissed me saying it was a direct order. I walked to my bed and just stared at the ugly area. I was scared to leave because I knew what I was up against here, and I hate the unknown. Whenever you get comfortable in jail or prison, they move you. I am not saying that you should ever be comfortable, but change is scary, especially in places like this. I had to figure out who the big mouth, the bully and the thief were once more. It was to start all over again.

Every unit gets to shop on a particular day, and ours had gone to commissary earlier that day. I had a bunch of junk food all over my bed. While I didn't really like it, I was an addict, going excessive in most ways. At that point in time, food had become my distraction. It was at least better than heroin.

I heard my name yelled again and the officer said, "Your escort is here McCarthy; let's move it!" "You can talk to your new best friend forever another time," she added, mocking us.

I was getting an anxiety attack, which I assumed was from withdrawal at the time. I just threw everything on my bed and wrapped the gray blanket around everything I possessed. I tossed the bundle over my shoulder and walked out into the hallway. I heard banging and turned around. The thief waved to me and shouted, "Are you leaving?" I nodded my head, tried to smile and left.

The officer was a somewhat pleasant escort – only, she wouldn't tell me anything about where I was going. This practice is normal when it comes to jails because they like to rely on the element of surprise. It seemed like an eternity walking down the corridor of the Rose M. Singer Center. Finally, I saw we were passing the cell buildings and heading to the annex, which holds all the dorms.

"No, I can't be going to a dorm, I have two violent felonies," I said. "Are you in here for a violent crime?" she asked. "Not this time, but that's not the point. I have been in Lock, SHU, and the BING in the past, so my classification should be high," I reasoned. She laughed and said, "Well I guess you ain't considered dangerous anymore, because your classification says low."

"Low! How can it be low? What does a person have to do to be considered dangerous?" I asked. I felt insulted that all my years of acting out were not even recognized anymore. My stuff started falling out of the blanket. The more I tried to save it, the more it fell. My open cherry Kool-Aid had leaked onto all my clothes and was spilling on the floor.

"They gonna be mad when they see this floor," the escort said, referring to the inmates who worked as porters and maintenance. I could barely hold the weight of my belongings and sweat was pouring off me. I just kept walking.

Finally, we got to the building that was furthest away from my old bubble. I walked up to the new bubble where the officer asked me my date of birth and address. He then told me to find a bed and buzzed the door. I walked into an oversized trailer that held 50 beds. It looked like an army barrack.

I started making my way down 'the highway', which was the center row of beds. It was also the most undesired since it offered no wall and little movement. Fortunately, I saw a bed in the corner, which suited my purpose. I liked having walls as I could watch my back and concentrate on my front. I darted for it.

As I got closer, I saw mostly Hispanics. They were looking at me like I had three heads. I did look crazy, sweaty and shaky but it was not like I had any options. An aggressor (dyke) female said, "Nah, we ain't messing with that," and I stood frozen. What was I supposed to do? It seemed like a pretty close-knit group. They were choosy about who slept next to them.

All of a sudden I heard, "I'll move there and she can take my bed." I remained frozen while a black female gathered her stuff from the highway and told me to take her bed. This was why I feared going to general population when sick. I did not have my wit or strength. Until I got some headway, I had to let people get away with treating me like that. The anger, shame, and pain in my body and soul became so severe, I became uncomfortably numb.

Making a bed in the state I was in seemed like a triathlon. I dumped my stuff on the bed and lay on my side. I felt my body tremor but tried to rest. "I'm going to get you mother fuckers back when I feel better, all of you," I thought to myself. This thought was aimed at the world, not just my immediate source of discomfort. I felt that I didn't deserve the life I had. Then again, I realized I had done a lot of things I wasn't proud of.

I think I slept for an hour before everyone got up and the noise became intolerable. I sat up on the bed and was facing the bathroom. I tried to get up but I couldn't. I took a breath and pushed myself to get up and wobble to the bathroom. I figured if I did it quick, it would hurt less.

I entered the bathroom and saw all the stained sinks on the wall, where you have to touch a rusty button for water to come out of a dirty hole. There was only one slop sink that was used for everything, from mops to brushing teeth. One woman was brushing her teeth and the woman next to her was taking a wet towel and cleaning her private parts, while sharing the same faucet.

I hadn't gone to the bathroom for about 10 days, as far as bowel movement was concerned. That's not abnormal with dope fiends because we remain constipated when we use methadone. I sat down on a toilet with no doors, which was on the wall opposite the sinks. When I tried to do what would make me feel human, only a whole lot of gas came out. I heard some people make a few comments so I just went back to my bed and lay on my side again.

Soon, they would be calling for methadone. I just had to wait, tick-tock. Time passed slowly. We had to get breakfast, which meant I had to get up and be in the mess-hall, the main dining area. I don't like them because they have resulted in a lot of fights. On that day, I just sat there and watched my peers eat, as they made me sick.

They called methadone in the early afternoon and I got up like life had new meaning. I rushed to the line for the medication window. In the hallway to the medication window, there was an officer who talked a lot of shit and cracked corny jokes. Everyone sucked up to her because she was the officer-in-charge of the methadone line. She could alter your life by kicking you off. I stood in line for what seemed like an eternity. When I finally got to the window I handed the nurse my ID. She turned around, ruffled through some papers, and said," I don't have anything for you."

"What? How can you not have my methadone, I just came out of the infirmary?" I asked, exasperated. "Well they probably didn't transfer your records – you have to get your officer to call them," she said. I looked at the methadone officer and asked, "What am I going to do?" She mocked me by mimicking my "What am I going to do?" in a voice that made me out to be a whiny asshole. All the other inmates laughed on cue. I was furious and shouted, "Where is my methadone?"

Her response was a curt, "I drank it, so get the fuck off my line, and if you go to get stupid make sure you come hard." Once again the inmates laughed. As long as it's not them, it's cool.

I walked away and swore I was somehow going to make the

whole world pay for everything that had happened to me. I swore to myself I would never be a victim again. I had to lash out, not at the underdog. All these big mouths needed to be drowned in a toilet bowl. The timing was wrong and the fantasy was just a fantasy.

About two days later, I finally got my methadone. One of the favorites went up and pleaded my case with the head officer. She, in turn, called the infirmary and it was done, simple as that. I don't like asking for help. I know that even if you never ask for anything, when you really need help it falls on deaf ears. That hurts almost as much as withdrawal.

The next morning, I got up and went to the commissary. It's a draining chore because women take their food seriously. The woman that works in the commissary usually throws items and you need quick hands to catch them. You do have other people pick your stuff up off the floor and ask you if you need help carrying it. I always say no because that's opening a door I don't want open.

I dragged my bags back to the unit and put my food in the bucket under my bed. I made sure I spent the maximum allowed because I came to this unit twisted and had gotten no respect. I had to change that. Since I came here looking crazy, I had to start over. I resorted to the tactic where if you shop, the perspective from others is that you ain't no 'bum bitch'.

To me, the whole concept is funny. The fact that you got money in jail shows that you are a bum because you're getting handouts. It's not really your money. I wasn't even hungry but I had to represent. My hands still shook like crazy and I still had the weird feeling I used to get before a drug-induced seizure, minus the drugs. I didn't have the strength to do anything but lie on my side and feel my body quiver with hot and cold flashes. The bright side was I had food, so I was 'somebody'. That was a start.

When I walked, my legs felt awkward. They stomped like they didn't know how to work anymore. I had an officer taunt me in the main hallway, saying out loud that I wasn't in the army and I should stop stomping my feet. I don't like being picked on.

I was at a stage when I had lost control of everything, from my five-year fake relationship, to the college I was going to while on drugs, trying to have my cake and eat it too. Reality was I was getting older and weaker. I guess part of me unknowingly surrendered and knew that if I wanted my life to change, the only way was to change forever, without looking back. I made a promise to myself. If I ever got my health back and had a chance to live a better life, I was never going to do this to myself again.

Eventually, I started bouncing back. I got close to some people. When I say close, I mean I could stomach them. I actually liked talking to them at times. My fondest memories are of Peachy. She was Hispanic, doing time for gang-related crime.

While I liked operating solo, we would sit and trade war stories. We even competed to see whose life was worse. When you don't make an impact on this world or have nothing to show for your life besides horror stories, there is little chance that you will let the next in line outdo you.

I was pissed because while we were both HIV positive, she had been shot. I couldn't top that. We discussed ways to make weapons out of medication packets. What we came up with was little more than a sorry excuse for a razor. No matter how much bravado we shared, reality was we were broken.

I watched her doodle on her skin, with the razor we'd made. She would scratch in a word and I never bothered stopping her. I was a cutter as a kid. I knew the wound was superficial and she was not going to die. Besides, emotional damage was not something we could conquer at that time. All said and done, despite the tough shit we talked about, all we were really good at was hurting ourselves.

Some of us really have to feel the pain and consequences of our behavior to this extreme. Even if you don't care about life, don't like this world or yourself, you know you just can't go through this ever again. That, then, was the beginning of an end to a 30-year active drug user experience. I guess I should be thankful.

5.
St. Patrick's Day

I walked into the assigned cell and tried not to look uptight or fazed to other inmates. It shows you're concerned, which in turn, exhibits fragility. I learned long ago that no matter where I went or how bad the neighborhood was, I was never look to lost or new.

I walked in like I was going into my living room – climbed up the bars and propped myself on top of the brick wall. The wall was about four feet high. It meant to provide privacy, for when you have to take a dump in a cage. Some things in life feel more punishing than others, and having to use a bathroom in a cage is one of them. Not only is it embarrassing, it is emotionally draining; using the bathroom in front of people who talk so much and say so little.

Not known to me then, I was suffering from multiple ulcers, always feeling bloated and out of whack. Using a bathroom in public was an option only in a serious emergency. The stress made my stomach act up and it hurt like it was going to burst. Little did I know that drinking water in a jail built on a landfill was probably what gave me the bacterial infection, H Pylori. That, though, wasn't discovered for a decade, so back to the situation at hand.

I have seen women have sex in different positions on toilets, where their mouth might as well be giving the toilet a tongue bath. Them talking shit about someone passing gas makes me laugh. "Courtesy Flush," they would scream, when someone was having a bowel movement in a stall. I don't know if that was supposed to be a noise filter or a smell diffuser. "Courtesy," sure is a funny word to use in prison.

To be honest, while I tried to avoid being the target of comments and ridicule, listening to the way people messed with each other still struck a nerve. My physical discomfort made me feel tortured. At that point, I hated everybody and everything.

Intake in Rikers is the processing facility for women at the Rose M. Singer center. There, they check your status or your 'classification' to process you. Your housing can be based on how low or high it is; sometimes I think it's a crock. Violent behavior can be a basis of classification.

I believe it is mainly about how sneaky you are. For instance, if you absconded from a drug program, they might consider you to be high-risk. If you're a celebrity, either because of your profession, or on account of your crime, you go to a housing area for people they need to watch. They don't want something to happen to you in jail while the newspapers are watching.

Most of us are just addicts who look like monsters on paper due to our addiction. We are housed accordingly. It functions quite like Bedford Hills Women's prison, the receiving area for all female inmates doing state time for a felony, as opposed to a misdemeanor.

The authorities decide your classification, which can be maximum, medium or minimum. This is not just a matter of

what housing unit you get, it also factors in which prison you go
to. There are the disciplinary standards in each facility, which
can raise or lower your classification. Well, enough of that boring
stuff.

The Intake at Rikers is a large room, about the size of a gym.
It has cells lining the outer walls, one for each borough. The
middle of the room has an officer's station, like a kitchen island,
which offers view of more or less everything. Not that they care.
They might need to take mug shots and fingerprints; and they
prefer that if you die, you don't do it on their shift.

The design is meant to facilitate organization of incoming
and outgoing court buses. However, since buses don't make pit
stops, whichever borough you get arrested in, this is the place
for your guest appearance – the cell/pen/potato holding area
that you are assigned.

An exception to this rule is 'Why Me Pen?' This is what
almost everyone says, given that they have to wait there until
the situation is under control. You might also have to wait till
the next shift feels like walking you back to general population.
It's like a tossed salad, with inmates coming, going and just stuck
talking shit.

While I was in was the Manhattan court pen, on that day
it also served as the Upstate pen for prison. It held numerous
women. Most of us were going to Bedford Hills Prison, convicted
of felonies; some were frequent flyers, always violating parole.

Some of us know each other from previous prison visits or
the street. However, you usually get cuffed to a person you can't
stand, or one who doesn't even know you're alive. Some take
the dominant role and walk first, making you feel like a dog on

a leash following their cue.

I had control issues so I was already figuring out who might be a problem. I wish I could say it was my first time going through something like that, but it was not. I went through the same process around a decade ago. It was culture shock, shell shock, and what not.

I spent lots of time in special housing facilities such as the BING on Rikers, and LOCK and SHU, which is upstate. Of course, there are women who are crazier than me, more destructive and reckless too. I am not saying I was a 'gangster'. In fact, the reason I was always in trouble was that deep down I felt overwhelmed, scared and desperate.

To be honest, I was tired. While my anxiety was still a monster riding my skin, I wanted to go home early this time and do my time peacefully. "How was I going to do this?" I thought to myself. At the same moment, a bunch of women were being led into a cell across the room, the release pen.

I felt it was kind of ironic, going upstate to wear greens on St Patrick's Day. I looked across the hall at the women. They were waiting to go home, or back to the street? Who knew? What I did know was they were going to be free.

Suddenly, I saw my friend Vicky and I was happy for her. I knew her future did not look bright. However, as an inmate and a hooker, she was my peer. We all strive for immediate gratification, so I guessed I should be happy for her. She saw me too. We pressed against the bars and waved to each other. Our movement was slow, like we were in a trance, as we stared at each other. Then, she mouthed the words, I love you.

I don't indulge in love talk crap. Only, I cared for her and she brought happiness to my life when I needed it most, as a friend and comedian. I usually try to make people laugh as a way of getting accepted and to serve as distraction in tense moments. For once, I met someone who had me rolling with laughter on a regular basis. While we waived, we had a sad eyes connection. Deep down, I think we both knew we had hard roads ahead.

Vicky was my opposite in many ways. She was very sexual in nature and was always smiling – until she got picked on – then she shut down, I was not sexual at all without my drugs. I was always racing to do something so I wouldn't have to stop and think. She was my comic relief when I came back from working in the laundry. She was broke and didn't want to work in Rikers but who could blame her? What do you do when you make change for an hour's work, not even a dollar?

I worked to stay busy and also to get in shape, thinking if and when I fought, I should be able to handle myself. I folded sheets in a women's jail all day, so do the math. That's a lot of arm work. I figured I was ready.

Vicky had gone to church regularly and even had a bible on the table where we sat. I used to mock her and say, "Do you read the bible between blow jobs on the street?" Deep down, I was jealous of her faith and hope, and her swearing that Jesus was going to fix things. What do you know? She was right.

I tried to get her to take the two years like me, which we both were offered. Although we had just met each other, we had a lot of common ground, which included drugs and co-dependency. I looked at life a lot more on the dark side, figuring I had to create my own reality based on strategy, whereas she was happily dependent on religion.

When you realize your plan of action in life sucks, you are in jail, and everything you tried to create and believe is a lie, deep down you know it never felt right. Only, it seemed like a plan at the time.

6.
Building 101

The dorm was shutting down because of health code violations, owing to which they were moving me into a building. No big shock, really. When we were told to pack our belongings, many women started panicking, saying things like, "I can't go to a cell" and "I need to be in a dorm." I was thinking I'd happily go to a cell because that was the best possible scenario for me – I could be alone.

I knew the dorm/trailer was a mess. The water that came out of the sink was grey. If you looked out the windows you could see sink holes in the not-so-lovely grounds. Yes, this was the fabulous landfill called Rikers Island. This was where all the 'bad' people went.

Fact that they built a jail on garbage shows how much the city cared about those inside. Pipes ran through the land-filled ground to provide us with drinking water. Do the math. When we went to court, traveling over the bridge to get to Queens, the smell was horrible.

A world in itself, it's not as physically dangerous as the men's side. After all, there are considerably fewer instances of women killing each other in jails and prisons when compared to men. It's still jail, though, and it serves as quite a culture shock.

When you're on drugs, there are times when you run the streets with the worst of the worst. You have drugs to distract you. Inside the slammer, your distractions are gone. Just being drug free is a culture shock in itself.

There is a lot of sex and corruption in jail. While there are some honest correctional officers, some others make it look bad for all. A few officers have their inmate flunkies to do their dirty work.

Flunkies in Rikers were the regulars, the frequent flyers. Jail had become a second home for them. Sex, drugs and money went hand in hand. Often, correctional officers were the ones bringing in contraband.

At that point in time, a Newport in Rikers went for $10, because inmates were no longer allowed to smoke. Why take a risk with drugs when you can make money through tobacco?

A correctional officer could bring in cigarettes. It was not illegal until it involved profit on the black market. Who better to do the hustling than the inmates under them? A pack of cigarettes can fetch $200. Even with taking shorts, it is still a big payoff. You could probably put a contract on someone for a Newport if you looked hard enough.

I was happy to go to a cell. I moved into building 101 and experienced, what felt like déjà vu. I had visited a similar building a decade earlier. When I had walked in, some woman shouted, "New jacks", real loud, like she was making an announcement. "New jack motherfuckers," followed. Eventually, we ended up fighting in the shower.

This time, the welcome was less hostile. Only, I guessed I was in for another anxiety attack. There were around 50 women in all. Besides the fact that I was the only white person, it was plain to see there was a shortage of chairs. It reminded me of a low budget 'jail' movie where someone came and claimed your chair or sneakers, and you had to fight.

Reality was it was not a movie. My mind was racing on how I could integrate with the building's existing occupants. To add to the obvious problem, some women felt entitled to sit with their chairs doubled, or even tripled, by stacking them.

I stayed in my cell the first few days because I never knew how to approach situations like those. In some way, I knew there was a disaster waiting to happen. I had lost faith in the human race a long time ago. I knew if I went and asked for one of their extra seats and they came out hostile, I would fight. Once I get that adrenaline rush which comes from anxiety, my hands shake and I can't eat anyway.

Sometimes, fighting felt better than arguing. Nervousness in just asking someone for a seat might seem strange to most people. However, what some consider 'no big deal' can make a mess of me, physically and emotionally.

I was a control freak due to fear and anxiety. The situation at hand made me feel like self-combusting. If I don't get into a fight, the anticipation of the possibility is even worse. Imagination can be a mother fucker, given that I always anticipate the worst.

The first few days, I kept to myself, in my cell. They brought food to the building; I came out only to eat. Finally, I managed to claim a table by getting other new jacks to sit with me. I always attracted odd-balls because we were not in synch with the swag that most others seemed to demonstrate. We gravitated toward each other and tried to laugh our pain away.

Our round-table of unhappy hookers was a piece of work. I acted like the leader. When others asked questions about me, I would put myself down with jokes. My mindset at the time was, "Hey, don't agree with me, though; I only allow me to hurt myself."

The 'modest' approach was part of my mask. By never claiming any type of status, I could concentrate on tearing down the character of others. Why? I don't know. Maybe, when you are not in a good space with yourself, it is simpler to focus on others.

One of the women at our table, Vicky, amused to no end. It takes a lot to impress me and I only laugh at my own jokes. This woman was unique – overly sexual and always with a bible. The first thing she said to me was, "I am a prostitute but I never sucked dick in my life." I didn't know whether to laugh or think she was crazy. "Really, is that so?" I wondered out loud, adding, "Care to explain?"

Vicky was very theatrical. She bit her bottom lip sexually, gyrating, showing her techniques in seduction, and said, "Once I put it on them, once it is over, they give me whatever I want." She continued to say, "They just give me whatever I want and throw money my way – I never have to give up no pussy." "Yeah right, then how come you're broke now?" I laughed and asked.

She was half-black and half-white, which should not be important. In Rikers, though, everything can be subject to ridicule. She told me she used to talk to some other women there, and when she told them her mother was white they treated her differently.

I had managed to orchestrate the closest thing I could get to a 'comfort zone' in jail, trying to get control without recognition.

What you have, who you know, or what you would you do for a Klondike bar is the basis of just about everything in prison. The sad part is if you are broke, you are labeled a bum. There were a lot of cool people there who were broke – they weren't planning to go to jail. It never made sense to me that some people got money from the outside and got to do their time a whole lot better than inmates who were broke. Does that sound like equal punishment?

Then again, a good lawyer can make you avoid such situations completely. Money talks in most scenarios. Many 'frequent flyers' are in cahoots with correction officers, either in corruption, or in knowing just whose ass to kiss. In some cases, they know each other from the street. Some of them are even related. Just getting toilet paper can be an event. They keep it in the officers' station and pass it through a little hole. You have to politely ask, "May I have some toilet paper please?" Getting ignored is common.

Birds of the same feather flocked at just about every table. There were 'dykes' and 'aggressors' at one table, which was not the norm – they are usually competitive with each other. There were several 'fake' gay women trying to act like men, so they could use others for supplies from the commissary. I guess if women cater to scrubs on the street, some assume that position in jail as well.

Hispanic women who spoke in Spanish occupied the next few tables. They kind of kept to themselves, like the rest of the world didn't exist. The 'shit-starter' table, with bullies looking for someone to pick on, was right next to ours.

We were the only table with a mixture of black, white and a Hispanic. We shared a common ground, we were all hookers.

One thing that got on my nerves was when my table glamorized crack. While we can joke and have delusional lives that we don't mind sharing, when someone tries to make crack smoking sound smooth, I thought they sounded stupid.

I am a dope fiend by nature, but I was also a garbage head. I was open to doing any drug as long as it put me in an altered state. Although crack was not my favorite drug, it was behind my recent downfall.

I had a boyfriend who was sneaking around, smoking crack. I initially figured he was with another woman. If I couldn't get through to him on the phone, it made my life miserable. When I found he was doing crack, I chose to be part of it rather than not. It started as a way to control him, but backfired. I let the drug take me to a place where I had never been. My boyfriend served as no more than a get-high-partner. A lot of people get confused about what a relationship is really supposed to be. Back then, I wasn't conscious of the fact that it was a hostage situation for both of us in that relationship.

Sitting at the table, I would listen to conversations of people sitting at surrounding tables. That was the only time I was quiet, when I was studying others. All day, I would hear racist comments aimed at the TV. During the show, Ghost Whisperer, one of the dykes went, "Yo, only crackers be seeing ghost," like it was a logical statement.

I know white people, as a race, are far from perfect. However, when I hear someone else saying derogatory things about them, it's like a knife in my nervous system. It wasn't a onetime thing. Some other references included, "She fought like a white girl," "She danced like a white girl," "She had a white girl's ass, called no ass at all."

How I felt was this. If y'all hate whites, it makes us enemies, right? Two seconds later, you ask me for potato chips. I couldn't even say, "Why do y'all say this," before a black woman would say, "What you mean, y'all?" Apparently, it was against street law to use a pronoun when speaking about blacks.

It seemed there were a lot of rules when it came to addressing blacks. Why, then, was it was okay to call whites honkies and blue eyed devils? Even if I was not a target of the remarks, I took everything personally. When I said something and the person bothered to reply, I would hear, "You ain't white, you black." Was I to treat that as a compliment? Why couldn't I simply be me? My anxiety was overwhelming, to the point where I had to do something to feel a release. Fighting was how it usually ended. When you feel uncomfortable in your own skin an don't know why life feels like punishment, it is easy to want to put a face to that anger.

The main reason I used to cut myself as a child was I could identify the source of the pain. It actually hurt lesser than the inner turmoil. Acting out was not being tough but reckless. Injuries I sustained were unimportant compared to my inner demons.

Don't get me wrong. Being white wasn't the only subject of animosity. Nobody was exempt from racial, pigment-related or just plain mean remarks – light skin, dark skin, nasty, broke, and so on. I think most of us had no true identity. Everything was superficial, based on false pride and ego.

You can say almost anything on the inside. If you say it with conviction, someone will believe it. Sex is a regular   pastime for a lot of women in jail. Prison is out of control as far as sex scandals and commissary hoes.

Rapes and sexual trauma had destroyed my sex drive. I sold my body for a major part of my life and felt ugly most of time I was at 'work'. I guess I was angry because some people seemed to be happy in jail. I didn't know how to be happy without drugs. Sometimes you hate someone for no apparent reason. People who were hurt went on to hurt others. I didn't fraternize sexually – I was a hateful person and didn't even see it.

Despite the fact that I was my own worst enemy, I did not like being a victim in any way. My coordination was returning. I went to work. The money was a joke, but it kept me busy. My senses told me I wasn't up to drama this time around.

When you're in the slammer, timing can be everything. In frustration, I tried to manipulate the manipulators. It was a simple plan, being that it is about survival of the fittest, meanest and loudest.

I had a 'paid audience'. My 'shopping' implied I had money in Rikers, which actually meant I was spending someone else's money. Never the less, money in prison makes you win an instant popularity vote. Everyone who dismisses you at first is suddenly interested in your jokes and life story. While it's plain to see these friendships are all about convenience, I figured a fake comfort zone beat a real struggle.

This might seem shallow or maybe I'm taking myself too seriously. Once, I sat there listening to two prostitutes glamorize crack. They acted like working the streets was fun. Both of them were in denial. They worked on the street in a rough part of the Bronx, but still tried to make it sound peachy. They   sounded delusional. One of them pissed me off. I think she felt the same about me.

One day, she said we should stop making fun of people behind their backs. I was like, "What would you rather do; talk about crack all day?" Sure, talking shit about other people is lame, but in my mind, it beat lying about drugs being fun. I knew from experience. Not being real about what drugs did was a crock.

I would not give out my commissary on command but I had things that some of the women wanted, be it coffee or a honey bun. If someone was trying to get a free ride, I was going to make them earn that shit by being my 'yes men', within limits.

I would bring enough to the table, literally and figuratively, so as to keep my surroundings in some kind of control. I am not saying we didn't care about each other at times. However, friendships in jail rarely go very deep because of circumstances and masks. People promise to stay in touch. The one you thought didn't like you writes you a letter, and the one you thought was your best friend, you never hear from again. I did what I felt was necessary, during when I felt I was being warehoused.

'Two for Ones' is a loan-shark jail hustle. The basis is you pay back double of whatever you borrow. I witnessed a woman sell her engagement ring for a pack of cigarettes and a bag of Lays potato chips. Fact of the matter was most of us were broken and beaten down with a lack of impulse control, which led to several bad decisions.

Even though I had come out of the infirmary five months ago and had kicked heroin, methadone and Xanax, I felt like a walking corpse. One of the many downsides of living a lie is when reality hits, it hits hard.

I tried to balance school, gym, drugs and working on Craigslist as a prostitute. The change hit me like a sledgehammer. I did not like what I saw. All I had left, that was worth anything, was my ego. If I lost a fight at that point, it would devastate me. It felt like playing a chess game.

When you ask for toilet paper, you'd better hope the officer is in a good mood. Once you lock in your cell, it's a wrap. Some inmates use toilets to keep their soda cold. I have had officers tell me I could wash my clothes in my toilet – they were dead serious.

I loved Vicky's company, but she was lost and couldn't decide if she wanted to talk about sex, drugs or the Bible. If crack head held sway over her, she would be a happy-go-lucky crack head.

Vicky had her ways because even though she was full of it, she was funny. That was something I needed around me to ease the stress. She would go to the officers' bubble, ask for toilet paper, and get it easily. I would go ask, "Can I get some toilet paper?" and get ignored most of the time. Finally, I would say, "Can I get some goddamn fucking toilet paper?" The usual response was, "No! Not by asking like that!" "Well, at least you heard me this time," I'd add.

Vicky knew how to get her way by using her signature moves. Besides being funny, she had no problem sucking up to officers. She would go up to the dispenser and say, "Hey Ms. whoever, I like your hairstyle, you be rocking it," and stuff like that. Then, she would squeeze in a, "Can you please give me a little toilet paper, pretty lady?"

Next thing, I would see a stream of toilet paper pushed through the slot, and she would take the whole roll. I would laugh my ass off. She had a gift of making the toilet paper into a hat that looked like a turban, which she would wear all night. One day she yelled, "White Power!" I almost choked and froze. "What the fucks are you doing?" I asked her, given that I was the only white woman in the building. She said, "My mother is white," and laughed. I was waiting for fireworks, but

All I heard was, "Oh really, where's it at?"

Since she pushed boundaries I would never push, I guess it was funny. Problem was she was not a fighter. The bully table picked on her a few times. It was easy because she was always in the spot light. I would sit there and watch. Unless someone jumped her, I stayed out of it. I felt bad because although she was someone who made me smile, she was not tough, and I could not fight her battles for her. I, after all, had my own demons.

When she was on a roll, she sexually harassed officers by messing with them while they did rounds, saying stuff like, "You sexy chocolate mother fucker." I would become hysterical because they did not know how to respond – it was a role reversal of sorts. When she sucked up to officers who were in the bubble, usually women, I felt like barfing. The upside was she was able to get what I couldn't.

When she eventually opened up to me, I found out her story was far from glamorous. She had a pimp who rode a bicycle with a basket he stole from a Chinese restaurant. He lived in abandoned buildings to get squatters rights. Vicky went to church faithfully. Even with my regular dose of sarcasm, she felt Jesus was going to fix things.

Vicky and I were in on the same charge, sale of drugs. We were addicts, not dealers. At times, addicts do stupid things. Suddenly, as far as society is concerned, they become dealers.

Both of us were offered two years. She just could not accept going to prison. She said she was going to pray and fight the case.

With my history, I knew I would not beat anything. I was just getting through the rapid detox so I could face the music. I asked her to do the time, thinking we might do it together. She said it was going to work out for her and she had faith. I cracked a Few jokes at her 'faith'. She remained undeterred.

Some days later, I saw a new woman walking around. She seemed Spanish and must have been in her early 20s. I noticed multiple scars all over her face and chest. I figured she was trouble because she was smiling all the time. I thought, "What the fuck is she so happy about?"

A few days later I came back from work and saw the scarred lady sitting at our table. I called Vicky over and asked, "Why is she sitting there?" Vicky told me the woman's name was Zolo and she was real cool. I don't know who I thought I was; I felt I had to go and assess her.

"What happed to your face?" I asked. Instead of telling me to mind my fucking business, she was more than happy to explain her whole life, which consisted of her 'sugar daddy' giving her money to do something positive. She bought crack instead and was embarrassed to tell him. She came up with an idea and had her friend slice her face, to make it look like someone robbed her. Her friend did it without any problem.

The scar on her face made it look like she was a victim of a serious attack. My cynicism and being judgmental faded away. I asked her what happed to her chest. She smiled and said a customer stabbed her. He paid her $15 for a sexual act and said he was not satisfied, wanting his money back. She was on crack and didn't want to give it back, but agreed she would return half. When she short-changed him by $2.50, he stabbed her in the chest, thrice. She woke up in the hospital and had to undergo an open-heart surgery.

I was dumbstruck when I finally realized why she was smiling so much. She was not able to let herself feel anything, and she became detached in the process. My two original women at the table started telling her she just needed to find the right people to get high with and I was irate.

How could they tell her, a child in my eyes, things were going to be better by doing drugs in the future? I felt they were stupid. While I might be crazy, even I know doing drugs doesn't end on a happy note.

At that point, I realized I needed to change. Women like those needed help, not new get-high partners. Her mother had been a crack whore who had abandoned her, never really giving her a chance. However, she was still alive, and I felt there was always a chance.

We were waiting for Vicky to come back from the hot pot. She was making some jailhouse Burrito recipe that was nasty, but everyone was ready to eat. Zolo was rocking and smiling. She seemed to be getting over excited, like a dog that wants to get out the door right before going on a walk.

Someone commented "Yo, check it out; she is doing the crack dance." This, supposedly, is a way of making fun of people who lose their sense of inner balance and have impulse control issues; so bad that they get hyper, and it is not a pretty scene. She was still smiling. It was because of the food that was coming. It was her substitute for drugs and drugs were her substitute for love. "No, it's deeper than that," I said.

7.
War Stories (2012)

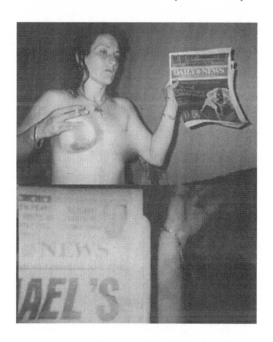

When I found out the medical examiner, the one who had been between my legs about a decade ago, was in a hospital around the corner from where I lived, it felt weird. It was kind of like you searching for your family for decades, only to find out they lived next door the whole time.

Even though the case was over and I had served my time, I wanted answers. My ex-boyfriend had overdosed while I was in prison the first time around. I knew he had no family or money.

I assumed his body went to Potters Field. It's quite a job, trying to get information about a poor person who dies, someone who was never on social media. It's like they never existed.

When you are not comfortable with a computer in this day and age, where navigation is vital, it feels like you are a mouse in a maze. It can get rather frustrating and intimidating because you are in a new element.

On that particular day, I was trying to find out what happened the night of my arrest for attempted murder. Someone informed me I needed to go to medical records for copies, so off I went. I walked into the office and the gentlemen behind the desk asked me if I needed assistance.

There was no easy way to ask what I needed to know. I just dived into the details, going, "Hi, about ten years ago I was brought to this hospital in police custody. I think they did a rape kit on me because I know that I was being examined down there." I went on to explain I was not interested in drama, and that I only needed my toxicology report to see what was in my system.

My lawyers always gave me the run around, even though I had a private one towards the end. The guy I was speaking with looked at me like he felt bad for me and said, "I am sorry, no toxicology was done." I was sure he was mistaken. How could they bring in someone unconscious, beat up and supposedly stabbed someone multiple times, without wondering about why there was loss of consciousness?

I got the medical records. I checked injuries to the victim and my injuries as well. Mine were minor in comparison. Records showed him to be my boyfriend. It was obvious they didn't even have a clue. It was also plain to see that my wellbeing was not on the mind of whoever was in charge that night.

When I had asked my private lawyer if I could plead self-defense, he said self-defense did not apply in the state of New York. I looked at him like he was crazy. How could they not allow people to defend themselves? Later, I found out that self-defense does apply in the state. Only, the wordings are different. The law in New York refers to it as 'justification', implying that the person who committed the act had no other option.

While my lawyer was private, he did not want to go to trial. He would then have to carry out research and go through all available information. Since I was not one of his high-paying clients, he wanted me to go the plea way. The records finally said something that made me happy – they showed I made a statement saying that I was attacked. They documented that at least. That, though, was the extent of my version on paper. I thanked the man. He wished me good luck. I left and was walking along Morning Side Park on the way to my house, when I saw an ambulance. I don't know why, maybe I still wanted an explanation, so I walked up and interrupted their conversation. I asked, "Yo, if you went to a crime scene that involved a stabbing, and the woman who did it was naked, beat up and seemingly unconscious, would you do a toxicology?"

The guy I directed my question to said, "No. For all we know, she might be drunk, and those tests cost money." He continued to tell me there are several domestic violence cases where people have blackouts on drugs and alcohol, and that's for the cops to figure out. Their job was just getting patients to the hospital.

What could I say? I was trying hard to change my life.   To

me, part of change was facing the truth.

The next day, I was right back at the same hospital. Incidentally, it was a hospital I had visited for years, as far as getting HIV treatment and meeting other health specialists was concerned. I was going back to the orthopedic doctor. Even though he didn't want to help me get an MRI for my neck and shoulder, my HIV doctor had ordered it so I could find out what was wrong.

I could not take any other pain medication besides Motrin because I was in recovery. However, I was in pain for over a year, from an injury I got while playing basketball in prison. Insecurities can make you try too hard, and that's what I did once I got clean in jail.

I was playing basketball, which I did in my own way. So what if I didn't know how to break-dance while I bounced a ball, like some of the other women? I had my own signature move. I would turn my back to the opponent, and shoot backwards, over my head. I am actually pretty good at it. There I was, tilting my head back for the twentieth time that day, when I felt something crunch. Immediately, I knew I was in trouble.

I went back to my housing unit and lay in bed, hoping it would be like the old days, and I would laugh it off when I woke up. The next day, I couldn't raise my right arm. It was like it wasn't connected to my brain anymore. I spent months being handcuffed and shackled, going to get physical therapy in another facility. It was a crock of shit and I couldn't wait to get home, to get the healing underway.

My arm had come back into existence, but it was not the same. My shoulder and neck remained in pain. I couldn't turn my head. When I raised my arm, pain shot across my right collar bone. The first time I went to an orthopedic doctor, it took about three to four hours to see him, despite having an appointment.

With his smug attitude, he asked me what was wrong. After I explained, he looked at the X-ray and said he saw no fractures. I was very frustrated. I knew my arm was still attached to my body and it was not broken, but something was wrong. He went on to say I was not young anymore, adding that MRIs were expensive.

Finally, I said, "Do I look like the princess from Princess and the Pea?" I continued to tell him I did not lead a sheltered life, and if I was saying something was wrong, it was.

He went on to say HIV medications did things like that sometimes, and it enraged me. If he had done his homework, he would have noticed I was on Interferon, a very strong medication. It makes your joints inflamed, to make your white blood cells work harder. If he was trying to bullshit his way around, he should at least have been good at it.

I felt it was personal. I was tired of feeling like a lowlife. At a time when I was contemplating killing myself, I got free drugs such as Methadone and Xanax without problem. When I was trying to change and get real help, it seemed hard as hell to get straight answers.

I calmed down and thought to myself, "Maybe I am overwhelmed and reading into it the wrong way. When he sees my MRI, I am sure we will figure it out together." Again, I waited for hours. I couldn't help but smile when I finally I saw him. It was partially because I was possibly going to get answers and help, and partially because while he had not wanted to help, my other doctor made the MRI possible.

In anger, he said, "You should not have had this done; all you have is fibrosis and bursitis." He went to say something else but I tuned out. My heart sank because I was back to square one. "Doesn't that mean something?" I asked, still a little hopeful. His reply was, "Why should tax payers pay for your MRI?" I was dumbstruck and it felt like time froze.

I was used to physical fights. They were a norm because of psychological, emotional and environmental factors. Situations like that one with the doctor hurt more. You feel like the people who are not supposed to help you hate you, and you don't know why. I resorted to my old behavior and cursed at him, even calling him Doogie Houser. I said other nasty stuff and passed some sarcastic comments, trying to hurt him in return. At the end of the day, I was at a loss because it solved nothing.

By the time I got home, I hated the world and my life. Luckily, I would be damned if I was going back to drugs again. I could not live like that. If I used drugs, I would be going through the same process over and over again. I wished to build a life that felt safe, and maybe, even happy.

Usually, there's a lot of shame in living a life like mine, simply because no matter how you try to analyze it, it remains horrible. Was I wrong? Was the world wrong? Was my family wrong? No matter what, I was not happy in my skin or in the world. The supposed civilized part of society was starting to look sketchy.

Another thing that became painfully clear to me was that people who had degrees and prestige were not necessarily good. Once you get used to being considered a lowlife, you almost start accepting it and can even try to define yourself with it.

I was starting to see I had sold myself short. Most of the women who were around me during my childhood were very well educated. They figured they were the power players because they controlled whatever little they could. It could be because they had money to make other people squirm, or because their education made them feel intellectually superior.

I decided it was time to get on my job and make something of myself. I didn't like being a pile on. A few days later, I had to go see a judge to check if I was eligible for SSI. While the Healthcare (HASA) HIV services help, part of the bargain is applying for SSI. This way, the state picks your case, and the city does not have to pay.

I was sick of being on welfare and SSI, but I was not about to try and get fast money again. While I'd applied, I was denied and was asked to appeal. I had to do what my caseworker told me, so I went to see a judge. I walked in and it felt weird; like I had committed a crime. There was a court typist who sat there and typed like an electric typewriter. A man with grey hair, who could have been as old as my father, was sitting on a podium, like he was the God that got to decide my fate.

"Do you have anyone representing you?" he asked. "No," I answered. I felt my situation was fairly obvious. I was on SSI before the arrest. Unless whatever they thought was wrong with me earlier vanished, I didn't understand the uncertainties. I felt if I had HIV, Hepatitis C and PTSD, which should speak for itself. Maybe I was imagining it, but he seemed to draw out his questions like he didn't really want answers. "So, Ms. McCarthy, I see you have been on public assistance for a long time," he said, stressing on the 'long'. It was not the first thing that got me defensive. Instead of going there trying to get disability, it felt like a battle. "Well," I responded sarcastically, "I have had

AIDS for a long time."

He went on to say, "I bet you even worked off-the-books." I replied, "Yeah, I was a hooker, it was a real peachy life, you should have been there. As a matter of fact, I traveled the world and the seven seas with all the extra money."

He told me not to say anything unless he asked me to, to which I said, "Do you think I like coming here, trying to prove how damaged I am? Do you think it feels good to try and figure out what is wrong with me, to plead that I am not fit enough to earn a living? Do I look like I'm happy?"

There was a moment of silence and the lady typing looked up at me for a second. The judge went, "You are in school, though?" I said, "Yes, because I am trying to build a life for myself; it is not easy, but I'm trying". After a few more unpleasant back and forth statements, I said, "I am just doing this because I have to, HASA makes me apply," and stormed out.

My application's denial came as no surprise. It was alright. since he made me feel like shit, I was coming back to win (win what, I don't know). I guess it's just a control thing. I was angry that doctors weren't helping me. It seemed I was made to feel like nobody in every possible way. I didn't understand it. I didn't get high anymore, and I didn't want a hand out. However, I needed help. I could not do it on my own. I learned quickly that you have to become your own hero and choose your battles wisely.

8.
Blackout (1999)

I jumped up because I felt pressure between my legs, like someone was raping me. Instead, I saw a white medical jacket and realized a medical provider was examining me. Believe it or not, I went back to sleep.

Considering I was being examined, with my legs spread by some kind of doctor, most people might think I would be startled, demanding to know, "What are you doing between my legs?" Owing to my lifestyle, I figured I was safe, and it was all that mattered.

My life never had an illusion of safety or security; my animal instinct was well and truly alive. The main flaw in my paranoid animal instinct was the drugs I craved. They were as important as the oxygen I needed to breathe. Later, I awoke in a cell and saw officers in the precinct right across me.

One of the officers noticed I moved and said, "It woke up." He laughed while another officer asked, "Did you do her property?" The first officer responded, "Fuck that white bitch. By the time she gets out of jail, every kid will have a cell phone in their lunch box."

I know it might seem unlikely for someone to remember that in detail, more so in my case, considering I didn't even know why I was there. However, you hear what matters to you. At that moment, I sensed danger due to the animosity.

I was a walking zombie for the most part. Even though I tried to hide from life with drugs, my spirit was dying. The only emotions I had left were bitterness and anger. When I got my drugs, I was one tough cookie. No, let me stop lying. Drugs were my crutch – they provided my alter ego a platform. If I was really tough, why couldn't I face life clean and sober?

I still don't know how I got from the crime scene to the hospital, or which hospital I visited. I don't even remember leaving the Harlem precinct and going to central booking in Downtown Manhattan.

"Your lawyer is here, she is waiting in the booth," someone said, directing me into a courtroom. All I had on were the hospital gown, hospital slippers and a skimpy pair of shorts. The gown was tied backwards, and I felt quite naked.

While I was still out of it, I noticed my arms were full of bruises, a few cuts and some scrapes. I sat down across from a white woman in a suit. She seemed angry. I figured she was a prosecutor. In a nasty tone, she asked, "Why did you do it?" "Do what?" I responded.

"Oh, you're trying to play dumb?" she asked, adding, "Why did you stab him 17 times?"

I felt a wave of shock come over me because this was not one of my usual Emergency Room visits, after which I could go, get high and forget life. Life just got very real, but it felt like a dream at the same time.

"Is he alive?" I asked. "Yes, lucky for you," she said. "Who beat me up?" I asked. Running out of patience, she said, "I don't have time for games McCarthy. Maybe Rikers Island will wake your ass up, and we can try this again then."

She was my designated lawyer. It was my first real taste of the legal aid system. My past encounters were no more than slaps on the wrist.

A misdemeanor is a criminal court case, where the highest penalty you can get is usually a year, typically spent in a local jail, and you don't go to prison. A felony, on the other hand, is a more serious crime and comes with stricter sentencing. Depending on the crime, you can get anywhere from one to three years, or even a life sentence. To serve time for a felony, you go to prison.

I was far from a jailhouse lawyer, I couldn't remember half my life, and everything seemed like a blur. Despite that, it was painfully obvious when someone did not care. My lawyer, by the looks of it, neither wanted nor planned to help me.

The shame I felt towards my life gave rise to a feeling of helplessness. I was looking at her like she was a God, with my life in her hands. It was scary because I saw the world hated me as much I hated life and myself. I was an addict and the most shameful part was I worked as a prostitute who had AIDS.

How can you defend yourself when you feel that most people consider you a monster? I had no real memory of the incident at that point. What I knew was it was a situation I could have avoided. All the warning signs were there. As usual, my addiction had taken over my gut instinct, and then, it turned out messy.

I felt I was being set-up at the crime place. The arrangement was I would go to his home and have sex. If he wanted me to stay longer than the usual time frame, I was to get drugs. This was not a norm for me because I did not do drugs with customers.

Do drugs when you have control over the scene, not when you are in someone else's domain. When drugs are involved, several things can go wrong, which can leave you vulnerable.

I usually managed myself by sticking to business. After getting paid, I would do drugs in my own time, in peace. Unfortunately, I had expanded my drug use and was dabbling with crack – a whole new demon.

When I got there, he offered me a drink. I declined and he looked frustrated. I asked him what it was and he didn't respond properly. He mumbled something and I said, "Nah, you drink it," laughing like I was too hip to get played. I watched him take the glass of liquid and place it on a shelf, which I thought was strange. Considering little in my life was not strange, I moved on to taking care of business.

I thought that by acting street smart and having a Rambo knife on my belt, I could chase away predators. Yeah, I was an interesting sight. However, when I worked for the escort service, the knife was not visible.

By showing I was not stupid I thought I had deterred the chance of an ambush. This was in a rough neighborhood and an even rougher building. I was tired. I was there instead of going to my escort service job. With the escort job, you have to sit in a car all night. You might not make anything because someone else is selling you over a phone. If there are no takers or if the phone girl is not promoting you, you might come home empty-handed.

Prostitution is essentially a young woman's business. Sometimes, we older women don't know when to throw in the towel. It's not because we like the job, it's because that is all we know. If you finance a drug habit by these means, it is hard to break the vicious cycle.

I know I used condoms but I also know several people are not going to look at that part. They are going to judge the fact that I have AIDS and think I was either trying to spread it or just didn't care.

I was always a judgmental person, trying to find fault in others, so I could feel less ugly on the inside. It didn't work. However, I know how I would have judged that particular situation if it did not involve me. I knew what I was in for.

The following few days were all about being sick and scared to death. I had lost my mind a long time ago and it was not letting me hide behind drugs anymore. I thought I was going to die in prison, of AIDS.

I finally got on the phone and called my mother, with whom I had a long and terrible history. While we did not share a nurturing relationship or healthy communication, I was desperate. I called, cried and begged. She and a friend bailed me out.

When I heard I was on the bailout, I felt too sick to walk or move, but it took me little time to get out the door to 'intake'. That was where they admitted and dispensed inmates.

You think you are walking right out the door and can feel those drugs making your pain go away. All of a sudden, your stomach feels like you are about to have the runs. So what if you haven't been able to go to the toilet for the last five days? Your body is going through something; I think only an addict who has experienced it would have a clue.

When they 'release' you, you don't get out straightaway. You get put in a cell for, what can be, up to ten hours. A captain 'white shirt' has to sign you out, and the time it takes can feel like forever.

What did I do once I was out? I went right to my enabler, got money for some heroin and went numb. I was not equipped to deal with life and I had a great excuse to hide again.

Supposedly well-meaning people asked me to research my case. Were they serious? I didn't know how to research. Look up similar cases, was the suggestion. That sounded impossible. The only thing I felt confident about that night was we made an arrangement and we had both fulfilled our parts. I had had sex with him after he paid me. Nothing should have gone wrong.

He offered me something to smoke. It was transparent, like shattered ice. When I asked him what it was, he said it was some new shit. I was stupid enough to smoke an unidentified substance with a complete stranger. Then again, I was an addict.

All I remember is feeling like I was sick and going into a seizure. How did I know what a seizure felt like, coming on? Well, I had drug induced seizures many times, from injecting cocaine. I never remembered anything afterwards, so it didn't matter. Those experiences were not really part of my memories.

I use to hear from my roommate that I had seizures. I apparently did all kinds of crazy things when I came out of it, like run out of the apartment naked. This would happen because I had seizures in the shower while using drugs.

Back to the incident at hand, I woke up on the floor. He was kneeling over me, telling me to drink water because it would make me feel better. It was the same cup that he used to offer me a drink earlier. I wanted him to get away from me so I drank it. I must have passed out soon after.

I woke up and my clothes were gone. He was sleeping. I figured he was trying to keep me trapped. I took his clothes and put them on. Just as I was about to leave, he jumped up and used my knife to threaten me.

He told me I could not leave and blocked the door. I knew my Rambo knife well. It had a jagged Christmas tree look. I wore it on my belt after getting attacked in the Bronx, where I lived. This guy was using my weapon on me.

I grabbed it by the sharp end. While it cut my hand, the element of surprise threw him off guard. I don't what happened after that. I don't know if he beat me up or if it was the cops. It didn't matter. I was the one going to the Supreme Court for attempted murder.

Next time I appeared in court, I saw the lawyer again. I asked her which hospital I was in for examination and what was in my system as far as drugs were concerned. I was looking for evidence that I had been drugged. She kept ignoring me. At one point, she went up to the judge and whispered something. Next thing I knew, the judge told me I had to get a private lawyer.

My legal aid jumped in excitement, going, "Yes!" I said to the judge, "I am on SSI and Medicaid, how I am supposed to pay for a lawyer?" He asked me how I got bail, to which I replied, "A friend borrowed some money." To that, he said, "Well, tell him to borrow more for a lawyer."

It felt like the world hated me. I knew I was a mess and did something wrong. The fact that nobody seemed to care about why I did it and what was done to me didn't seem right.

I think he was in the country illegally. He never came to court. Maybe he knew what happened and didn't want to be discovered for being a part of the insanity. I had an order of protection that did not allow me to go back to where he lived.

Part of me wanted to confront him and ask, "What happened?" There was no motive for me to stab him, besides being scared or in retaliation. Then again, why would I want to go back to a place that had altered my life? It was like a bad dream and I could only remember pieces. I got back to drugs and the second felony was to follow soon.

On the street, some guy came up and asked me if I was working. I was like, "Yeah, do you want to get high?" It was no more than a show of me being at an all time low in my life. I had just gone through a nightmare, which I was still fighting in court – all because of mixing drugs with business.

At that time, I was far-gone. I just wanted to be numb, no matter what the cost. I did not want to go to prison for something I couldn't remember. I definitely didn't want to kick my methadone. That's a harsh punishment in itself.

There, I had this guy saying, "Yeah sure, here's $40." It seemed too easy. I went into a subway station to cop. I talked to the dealer and his buddy, both trying to cut me short, Midtown being the place to rip people off. Just when I was debating with them, two undercover cops came from towards the station's exit, telling us to get our get our hands against the wall.

All of us dropped money and swallowed any drugs we had; trying to avoid giving them evidence. The clock began its tick tock immediately. I figured I was going to jail. I was sick already. My mind started racing.

I decided to make a run for it, running up the station's staircase. The male undercover, who looked like a Wall Street accountant, grabbed me by the back pocket of my jeans, since I was higher up the stairs. I felt he was going to yank me, so I turned around and kicked him in the groin.

Don't ask me where all that energy came from or what movie I thought was playing. When he went down, I descended a few steps and continued kicking him, telling the dealers to run. His partner, the one who looked like a secretary, came towards me. I thought I could backhand her, when a blast of, what felt like acid, hit my face.

I got down on the ground screaming, "Get this shit out of my eyes." Well, I guess some people handle pepper spray better than others. Whatever role I thought I was playing came to an abrupt end. I thought my face was melting.

The ambulance came and squirted my eyes, but I still had to go to a hospital to get my eyes flushed. When I could finally see a bit, I demanded to see a mirror to check how much of my face had melted. Then, as my vision normalized, I saw two uniformed policemen standing over me. I toned down and asked, "What happened?" I was playing dumb because I knew exactly what had happened. In any case, they didn't buy it. Soon, I was on my way to Rikers, in a cage in the front of a bus, with all male passengers in the back.

There was a black guy behind me, in another cage. These cages are either for special prisoners as far as the media is concerned, or for ones in protective custody. Once in a while, they put prisoners in them just to make room. While the guy in the other cage was talking a lot of shit, he was funny. He made me laugh, and under those circumstances, I felt obliged.

First, he was rapping, saying he was a black "Dennis the

Menace." Then, he became a black Santa Clause, who would supposedly come down your chimney and steal presents. I know that might not sound particularly impressive. Only, the situation was so out of control, his crudeness worked like comic relief. Besides, everything in life was bizarre anyway.

When we talked, he said he was going to jail just for a few days, adding that if I needed someone to talk to, I could call him. However, I didn't have a pen. I tried to remember his number in my head. When I got to Rikers, a female correctional officer told me to sign a paper on my way to the intake process. I took the pen and tried to write his number on my hand quickly, when the officer said, "Get your trashy white hand of my pen!" I went through another song and dance there as well. Luckily, it didn't end in injury.

Any time I complain about racism towards whites, all my black associates say I am living in the past, and that it ain't like that. I know racism is far from over. At the time, though, I could only see it from my perspective – a minority within the minority.

9.
Tough Guy (2002)

"McCarthy! Go to the library after the count because you have legal mail," the main officer in my housing unit said. At first, I was wondering what it could be. Then, I remembered I'd ordered a copy of my rap sheet.

I felt I had to let others know I was a violent felon. That way, they would think twice before messing with me. When I pleaded guilty, I was handed a lesser charge. Attempted murder had gone to aggravated assault, and then, it changed to first-degree attempted assault. It sounded strange to me. How do you attempt to assault someone? Throw a stick and miss? Go to kick their ass and slip in the process, before your leg makes contact?

Jokes apart, reality was harsh. I had gotten three and a half years for supposedly stabbing someone over 15 times. Whatever they wanted to call it was fine by me. It was like being the star of a shitty movie. I felt that since I was the supposed 'bad guy', I might as well run with it.

I planned to stage a scene, getting nosey people to read my rap sheet. I would ask them 'not' to read my shit, and then walk away. That way, it wouldn't seem obvious. I would leave it on my locker and curiosity would make them look, or so I hoped. Otherwise, I would have to pretend I didn't understand something and then get one of the jailhouse wannabe-lawyers to take a look.

I hoped my rap sheet showed what a psycho I was, because it sounded good inside. I liked the sound of me being a crazy white bitch. It definitely sounded better than an easy white vic. Vic stands for victim, and I don't like being one. I felt like a little kid who was getting a new bike and wanted to show off.

When I was in Rikers, some women said I was making my charges up. This used to happen behind my back. Only, my supposed friends couldn't wait to give me every detail, while they smoked my cigarettes.

One woman said there was no such thing as three and a half years flat, which meant a flat sentence. This was opposed to one to three or two to four years kind of sentencing. I was new to how these things worked. Frustrated, I said, "Well, tell that to my judge, Judge Mathis." How dare these women question my pain and stories?

I guessed they thought my life was easy or I was soft because I was white. Why did I have to do something to prove otherwise? For kicks, I explained to others how I assaulted a cop. I knew recounting the particular episode would give me the street cred I needed to make people leave me alone.

It was funny in a way. Both violent acts had been because of drug-induced insanity. That, though, remains my secret; there's no need to get technical.

I got to the library, which was also the place to pick up legal mail. I signed my name and the officer handed me a large envelope. I couldn't wait to get back to the unit, ripping it open right there, noticing it was thick. I started scanning the arrests to get to the impressive part. The prostitution and drug related arrests were anything but.

I saw a charge that said 'Assault with intent to disfigure/ dismember'. While I wanted to make an impression on my peers, I realized it couldn't have been me. I didn't dismember people. Next, I saw a charge related to firearms/weapons. I knew I didn't mess with guns. Although I should have been basking in glory, it felt weird. The rap sheet made me look like a psycho.

There was a feeling of uncertainty. I realized I didn't remember at least half my life because of drugs and trauma to the head. As a result, I couldn't confirm or dismiss anything with conviction. It felt like I was someone on TV, and my life was unfolding with every passing episode.

When I got arrested, I was on disability. I was suffering from dementia, which is similar to Alzheimer's disease. Upon being diagnosed, the doctor gave me the news like it was an achievement. He said, "Guess what, you're eligible for SSI now." Then, he wrote me my script for Xanax.

I was told I wasn't going to live for long. At the time, it didn't really matter. All of a sudden, I was having a change of heart. I was not dead and my life got very out of control. I did not like feeling stupid and not knowing who I was. I was used to feeling crazy. Once, I went to a psych ward and begged them to admit me.

Another time, I was having hallucinations, where I had an aerial view, watching myself talking to people. As soon as they found out I did drugs, they told me to go rehab. I would plead with them and say, "I need help; I am watching me from above; I am not in my body at times; I need help!" They dismissed me and told me to get off drugs.

When you're an addict or a felon, a sad part is your word doesn't mean shit. Now, people have excuses for how they've treated or neglected you in the past. You are no longer credible. That is the most dangerous part about someone who has a fairly stable environment – signing away your sanity – because you aren't taken seriously any more.

Not for the first time, I felt life was like a chess game, and I was losing. I had no real identity. At home, half of my closet had hooker clothes and the other half had thug gear. The latter helped me look tough while I copped drugs. I was trying to make money with one side of the closet, and was using the other to put on a different mask, so I could coexist on the street. Both sides were tattered, and I didn't like either.

Once, I was going to cop my drugs, when I saw some young black women hanging out on a stoop. I was wearing a Roca wear jacket with a big hood and Timberland boots. My red hair was showing. As I walked past them, I heard one say, "Look at this old bitch trying to look young." I hate to say it but I laughed. After all, she hit the nail on the head.

Even though I felt someone had used my identity, I could not help blabbing about it at the table in the library. "What does this mean?" I asked another woman. She started skimming through the 14-page rap sheet and we discussed it, with other people within earshot. Finally, I got up to leave, and I heard the officer yell "On the movement." That was the cue to head back to my building.

I had plenty to disclose, which should have made me happy. However, it was scary that I could have done all those things. If I showed others I got arrested for guns and for trying to dismember people and never went to prison, they would definitely think I was a snitch who worked with the cops.

I had sent for the arrest report of my dismembering case and was anxious for the next few days. I wanted to know what happened and I wanted to clear my name. It was weird. While I wanted to look tough, this was a little too much. I was ashamed that I looked like monster on paper. Deep down, I knew it wasn't me.

I sat on top of my locker and watched other inmates, categorizing them. That one's fake; that one's a thief; that one is a bully; and that there, is a bimbo, all in the officers' faces. It irked me to see this one bimbo smiling and sashaying her way up to the officers' station, twirling a piece of hair and laughing at the officers' corny jokes. She would repeat it every shift. I studied her and grew to hate her.

One day, I walked by and said something sarcastic like,

"Damn, you need your own post, since you're here all day." I expected her to be embarrassed. She came back like a firecracker and said, "I am going to stay being up here in their faces, and if I can get some dick, I am going to do that too!"

Whoa! I didn't have an answer to that one. Why did she bother me? I had to admit she was getting the attention I craved. The only way I knew how to get it was by acting out. To see her smiling and being happy in prison, it just kicked my shit up. She had everything I lacked, except a high IQ.

There was another woman I couldn't stand. She got five to 10 letters a day. I would wonder who would write to that bitch, and it made me feel forgotten. That's why I didn't like her. I would order things so they would call my name when mail came, and no one else was any wiser.

Back then, the only way I would have liked your company was if you were predictable, easy to control or more fucked up than me – in which case I would feel sorry for you. I didn't know why, but crowds bothered me. I did not like being in any kind of a line because it made me feel trapped.

When you stand in lines where everyone is loud and people keep cutting in, it gets to you after a while. I guess that was why lines bothered me. Simple things were hard to accomplish. The only time I felt relaxed was after a fight, and I didn't understand why.

I generally avoided the TV area. I knew I would get pissed off or see someone treat someone else badly. One day, I walked into the unit and saw everyone in a trance like state, staring at the TV. Nobody was talking or arguing. I couldn't help but go in and see what it was about.

What I saw was bizarre. Buildings were falling down and everyone was running. At first, I thought it was a movie, like King Kong or Godzilla. Suddenly, I realized it wasn't a movie. It was the World Trade Center in New York, going down. Even though we were near the Canadian border, the feeling was eerily strange.

It was like I was watching the end of world unfolding. From behind me, I heard a woman say, "Good, I hope they kill all those 'pink' people." I felt my inner rage and familiar feelings come back. The funny part was she was sucking an officer's pink dick up there, but that's beside the point. Life could be rude, vicious and hostile to whites in prison. Only, the whites that blacks target in prison are not the elite who run the show on the outside.

Women started panicking. Some were saying they were going to kill us because we were trapped inside. If it wasn't such a horrible situation, I would have laughed. I couldn't help being condescending and asked, "What makes you think they would want to kill us?" One kept rambling about how they were going to get us, to which I said again, "They don't want us to die, they want us to live." "We are not important enough to kill."

We were away from densely populated areas, in a two pigs and a cow town. I felt safe as far as becoming a target. However, the feeling of watching so much pain and destruction remained imprinted.

Growing up, I heard about slavery, both the World Wars and of the U.S. presence in Vietnam. I guess you never really get a feel of others' pain until it hits home. The Twin Towers going down was surreal. I couldn't believe it happened and was hoping it was a dream or a prank. I knew it wasn't.

Around two weeks later, I got the arrest report for one of my violent charges, one I did not remember. I wanted to see who used my identity. When I read it, I froze. The names were familiar. I saw a mention of Bleecker Street. Immediately, I knew it was not a case of stolen identity.

The document said I had sliced my boyfriend's neck with a box cutter, and that he needed plastic surgery. I knew he never got it because he was dead. He had given me AIDS on purpose. While I did not kill him, I did not know how to handle the situation. The arrest report said the argument started over a condom, which made sense, because I had a different fight with him about that. I just didn't know it had escalated to that level.

Then, it said, I got released on my own recognizance. How? Why? I remembered cutting my dead boyfriend and that was the last time I saw him. The document I was reading made me question my memory, life and story. Not much added up.

10.
AIDS and Confused (1990)

I felt hollow. I had not come to terms with the fact that my life had reached such a stage. I had to take on the role handed to me. I remembered when I was a teen and would complain about being bored – I wished my life were boring then. I came closer to the house and started getting nervous. Then again, what else wrong could possibly happen? I didn't think there was any other situation that could faze me.

If he decided to hurt me again, I didn't think he could do much besides kill me. I felt that might be easier than to live with the newfound reality. The way I saw it, my life was over; I had nothing to lose. There is a calming effect in knowing you're dying because the pressure of proving a point to anyone does not exist anymore.

I had just come from an STD clinic in Manhattan after waiting out the 'window period' to get an AIDS test. I told them, "I know I have it, there was blood and semen mixed!" They were not interested in my emotions. For them, it was no more than a medical test.

I had just found out I was positive and had a life expectancy of six months to, maybe two years, if I was lucky. Why did he have to take me with him? I would have been there till the end – he didn't have to hurt me. Now that my boyfriend was successful in infecting me, we had some unfinished business.

He said he did it so I would not leave him. I was never going to leave him. He didn't have to do that to me. I was scared to see his face because I injured him badly after the rape. It was a horrible day for both. I didn't see the extent of the injury because I had gotten him by surprise – the same way he got me. An eye for an eye is the way it goes on the street. When someone hurts or disrespects you, you have to stand your ground.

That incident was more than just disrespect. It was traumatic. When it happened, I shut down emotionally. I was in some kind of a robotic state as I planned my attack. I had never been as calm as I was at that moment; it was strange. At a time like that, you no longer weigh the situation or try to figure out who is wrong or right. Only, it felt so wrong that I shut down, like I didn't know how to process the situation.

I am a codependent person. I never like to give up on my relationships. The same holds true for crutches and distractions. However, this was different. I needed closure. If he wanted to report me, I would have known by then. Why did I not report him for giving me AIDS? The particulars don't remain clear.

I guess part of me still wanted to stay with him because I didn't know where else to go. My family was not supportive. If he opened the door, maybe we could cry and forgive each other. He would forgive me for his scarred face and we would live and die together, happily. I know, now, it sounds crazy. There was nothing there to romanticize.

It started to get ugly on a day I will never forget. We were watching TV and having our usual day, when he got up to go to the fridge. I noticed a patch of hair on the pillow, in the shape of his head, which got me to think, "He is only 22, why is his hair falling out?"

I asked him, "Honey, why is your hair falling out?" Without even wondering why I was curious, he quickly said, "It must be the new shampoo." While he took a shower, I laid back and thought about how we had been together for over two years. He was still sticking to his 'dancing job' story, but wouldn't get into details.

I noticed he had a real flexible schedule and never called his workplace. When I asked questions, he got defensive, saying I knew from day one that his job wasn't open for discussion.

About a week later, when he came out of the shower, I couldn't help but notice how much weight he had lost. When I saw him in the doorway, his silhouette did not look the same. "Why are you losing so much weight?" I asked. "I don't know, maybe it's the heat," he replied.

While I could not imagine what the real problem was, I decided it was time to stop playing and staying stupid. When he got dressed to leave, I acted uninterested, like I had my own plans. As soon as he left, I followed, staying about a block behind him.

It took a lot of work, following him from Jersey to New York, but that was our norm when we were together. On that day, we walked separately, and he was none the wiser.

Following him, I thought how stupid I had been, letting him get away with his secret life for so long. Even though his looks were deteriorating, I loved him. That's why it took so long to notice the change in his weight, and otherwise. I saw him every day, so the change kind of hit me in a flash.

I was on a mission. I still don't know what made me follow him. Whatever it was, it was trying to tell me something. In Manhattan, I followed him to 50th Street and Seventh Avenue, to a Bar called Stella's. I waited outside, for him to get comfortable inside. This way, he wouldn't be able to say he went in to use the bathroom. Stella's, by the way, was a gay bar.

Things started adding up. I was aware some guys were into the gay hustling scene. Since I worked in peep shows in Midtown before I was with him, I was hip to certain spots through word of mouth. I waited for about five minutes, which seemed like a lifetime.

Around that point in time, AIDS had hit the gay population. To be honest, there was little to no sympathy until it started hitting the entire population. Even I was ignorant on the subject, which changed considerably in the years to come.

I went into the bar and saw him with a man twice his age. He was getting very cozy. Both of them looked engrossed in conversation. I walked up and said, "Dancer, huh, I don't even want to know who gets on top. You're a fuckin' faggot." I walked out and he followed me, trying to down play the situation.

"You're a hustler? You know how many gay men are dying from AIDS?" I asked him. "Hold on," he said, "It's not as bad as it looks. I just let them suck my dick for money." "Oh, please!" I said, "That's what they all say," adding, "Tomorrow we are going for an AIDS test, and you better hope you're negative".

"Why don't you take the test for both of us," he said, "since we've been together for so long?" I should have read between the lines and realized he didn't want to take the test for some reason.

Suddenly, it made sense. Whatever he had, I had, because we never used protection. While we didn't have anal sex, logically, we would share the same STDs (sexually transmitted diseases).

The next day, I went to an STD clinic in Chelsea, Manhattan, near my mother's house. When I got tested, there was a considerable waiting period for results. For some time, he and I stayed sexually inactive and dealt with the tension on a day-to-day basis. When I finally got the results, much to my surprise, I tested negative. As far as I knew, that made him negative too.

I ran home and told him. He looked like he wasn't happy. Later, he confessed he had AIDS and was afraid to tell me. While this might sound stupid, I figured that if I didn't catch it after having unprotected sex for over two years, I was relatively safe for the road ahead too. I felt it was my duty to stand by my man. He was my new family. How could I judge him for making a mistake after I had worked in peep shows and as a call girl?

I changed my life when I met him, by starting work as a telemarketer. We got high on weekends, but it was not the heavy stuff. I did not insist on condoms because I didn't want him to feel ugly or undesirable. Part of my problem was I did not have a healthy sense of self. My life was tied to the person I shared it with.

There was little education about AIDS at the time. Most considered it a gay man's disease, or a disease from another country. I used to think it wasn't my problem. It is amazing how much your position and attitude changes on matters when the shit hits closer to home.

Deep down, I resented the fact that my life had changed. I didn't know how to care about myself by myself, so I went with the flow. Till date, I don't know why his hair was falling, because it is not common in people who suffer from AIDS. I got to learn about the disease the hard way.

We did not have anal sex. It never came up and I was not curious. We had sex doggy-style most of times. On that particular day, we were having sex. After being with someone for a while, you can learn their rhythm, and almost time them. He pulled out early, purposely, and waited until he was ready to ejaculate. He raped me anally, and did it at the last moment, making it like an ambush.

He was trying to say it was an accident, apologizing and saying he missed. In my head, though, I knew something had gone wrong. I was in a mixture of shock, pain and confusion. I jumped up and limped to the bathroom. I felt violated. I will never forget trying to wipe the area. Blood and semen were all over the tissue.

Even though some might think it was my fault for continuing sleeping with him, it is one of those situations you have to experience personally before you can judge. I had nowhere to go. I was the black sheep of my family. Who was I to judge when we all make mistakes? Besides, I was negative after two years.

For some reason, all of that lovey-dovey stuff went out the window at that moment. I started cursing him and saying things like, "What you mistake me for is one of those fags you fuck." I was still in the bathroom, trying to recuperate, when he said something that changed everything. Mixed up, he said he violated me on purpose.

He stopped acting like it was an accident, maybe out of anger arising from my insults. Finally, he said what I knew by then, "I infected you so you won't leave me bitch."

My mind shut down. I saw my jacket hanging on the door. I knew I carried a box cutter and it was in the pocket of that jacket. I got up. For once in my life, I was not anxious or stressed. I took the large orange box cutter out. There were different blade settings to choose from, and I pulled the full blade out. I picked a pair of pants from the hamper in the bathroom, put them on, and walked back into the bedroom.

I started packing my stuff. I had nowhere to go but it was as if some alter ego had taken over. "You didn't have to do that," I said, adding, "I was making love to you without a condom. Does that sound like someone who was going to leave you?"

While I carried on, almost monotonously, he didn't even respond. I think he saw a different side of me. I was not yelling or flailing my arms while I talked. I was packing, systematically. When I had gotten what I needed, he was walking next to me in silence. As I opened the front door, I pulled the box cutter out of my back pocket and slashed his face, from one side to the other, with the strength of a punch.

I refused to be a victim, at least not an obvious one. I promised myself nobody was going to get away with hurting me again. I had learned at an early age that if someone can hurt you physically and emotionally, they usually do. When I was growing up, as a child, my mother went through a terrible ordeal. She probably did not handle it in the best possible way, but she had two children. My brother was two years older than me.

When I was seven years old, she got multiple sclerosis. Soon, her life and marriage crumbled. She had gone to Ivy League schools, and then, she had to be on welfare. She couldn't work and, I hate to say it; she couldn't be much of a mother. She went through the norms to her best ability. As far as nurturing goes, it wasn't a factor in my relationship with her.

As a child, I had several weird ways to cope with anxiety. I started cutting myself at the age of seven and a half. When you are in the care of someone who is not stable, it can be a very scary way to live. When I was 12, my mother attacked me, because she had episodes of anger. By then, I was big enough, physically, and I shoved her back for the first time. She fell and broke her wrist. Guess what that made me? A problem child, packed off to a home for children.

There were a few other instances when I felt helpless or scared. However, your being crazy can make all the crazy people sane, and then, you become the monster. How fucking convenient.

Other than feeling violated, I think it was the feeling of betrayal that made me disconnect. The damage was done. My family had not taken me in even after finding out I was dying. My dad tried to look supportive but his girlfriend set the stage. My mother told me not to call her, and wished me the best.

With AIDS that he passed on to me, where could I go from there? I finally got to his place and rang the bell. His father answered the door. I felt ashamed that he let me live there and probably didn't know why his son's face was cut.

I asked him where he was and he said he was not there. I pushed past him and told him I was not going to hurt him, I just wanted to talk to him. He said, "My son is dead." I didn't believe him. I checked under the beds and in the closet. He said, "I am sorry, I didn't know he was sick." I sat down with his father and cried. "How did he die?" I asked. I saw him 90 days ago.

His father explained that his son had given up and stopped eating. He was sick, but not that sick, I thought to myself. I asked his father if I could take some pictures. He let me take the entire photo album, after which we said good bye. That was closure, but not the kind I anticipated.

I wondered if I was supposed to feel sorry for him instead of bad or angry. I didn't know how to react. He gave me AIDS so I wouldn't leave him. Then, he was dead and I was alone.

11.
Frenchy (1998)

I hated working the street. When you work for an escort service, you get delivered like pizza, and the phone girl does all the haggling; you just focus on your work. On the street, the whole world gets to see you standing on the corner, like you have nothing better to do.

I sucked at being a street hooker, no pun intended, simply because I was not aggressive. I felt awkward, trying to make it look like I was waiting for the bus. I hoped some guy would figure out I was working and sweep me off the street, and off my feet. That, though, was the real world, and not 'Pretty Woman', with Julia Roberts working her charm on Richard Gere. Reality was far from it. The clock continued with its tick tock.

I remember getting there in broad daylight. My dope habit had no boundaries when it came to feeding the belly of the beast. I stood there with my poker face, waiting endlessly. The more seasoned street hookers in front of the peep show tried to grab leaving men. One even stood in a man's path and brazenly asked, "Hey, you want a blow job?" She said it with the sexiness of a drunken cab driver. When she eventually got a taker, I was pissed.

Someone who looked African-American was standing close

to them, going, "girls, girls, girls." I figured the peep show had hired him to lure customers. A man walked past me, went up to him, and asked, "You got girls?" The black man put on a fake French accent and said, "Yes, would you like a blond, brunette or redhead?"

The probable customer, probably a tourist, said he wanted a blond. "How old?" the French businessman asked, like he had a stable full of women. I couldn't help but be nosey as hell, to make sense of the whole scene. You get to learn most things on the street the hard way. Once in a while, you learn by observing.

I think what I really wanted was to learn why I was not making money. How was the sweatpants wearing dude with a fake accent and rundown Timberland boots that looked like they belonged in the garbage, with their toes bent upwards, more successful than me? My insecurities and anger made me study that seemingly more successful person.

The tourist said he wanted a 16 year old. Quickly, he corrected himself, "An 18 year old, blond," he said. Frenchy was more than happy to oblige, telling his newfound customer that the girl would cost $250, and the room came at an extra $50. The tourist bargained with Frenchy, saying he only had $275. Frenchy said, "Okay I am going to give you a break this time, but make sure you come with the correct amount next time around."

He handed the naïve tourist a key and told him to go to Carter Hotel, just across the street. "Knock on door 219 three times before opening it with the key," he said. The tourist walked off, thanking him. Frenchy did not waste any time running down into the subway.

Frenchy made $275 for nothing, in no time, and I was   still dope sick. Tick tock, tick tock. The longer it took me to find a customer, the more awkward I felt due to withdrawal. Finally, one of my regulars grabbed my arm and we walked to the Dive Hotel. There was no need for words.

I did what I had to do and left the short stay hotel, heading for the subway. I saw Frenchy in the subway car but dismissed him. I had my life and power back; soon, all the pain was going to disappear.

The following day, I walked to my place of business and saw Frenchy back at his con game. For some reason, I felt I had to let him know I knew what he was up to. As I walked by, I asked, "Hey what's up con artist?" He was quick to respond, "What's up hoe who can't get paid?" meaning I was a slacker.

The street is a funny place because a thief feels superior to a hoe, and a hoe feels superior to a beggar – not necessarily in that order. With hookers, there are two kinds, those with pimps and those without. The distinction is important because a hooker with a pimp feels superior to a 'renegade', who is someone that operates independently. I worked on my own, which made me a renegade.

While I considered hookers with pimps as stupid blind followers, reality was drugs functioned as my pimp.

I remember the first time I had a run in with a pimp. I was working on a block, car hopping. What it entails is hopping in and out of a car. It does not pay well but is quick most of the times. I liked working after dark, so I wouldn't have to be seen or end up seeing anybody of importance. I didn't make eye contact with people because some people viewed it as a challenge.

People who are not happy with their lives don't want others

to look into their souls. I felt that way. One thing I did not do was rob tricks. I did not want to get killed. The probability of having bad nights were high enough dodging psychos and cops. Pissing off men in cars was a definite no.

I was walking around the corner when I saw a tall black man. He said, "Good evening" to me as I walked by. I smiled and kept walking. He added, "You have a pretty smile." I thought it made sense to be polite, so I said, "Thanks." All of sudden he blurted, "Bitch you are out of pocket, so break yourself!" I did not have a clue of what he meant, which might have been a blessing at the time. Later, I found out he meant my acknowledging him was a sign of disrespect to my existing pimp, because of which I then belonged to him, the new guy. That was their law.

I didn't know what he was talking about but knew it was not good, so I just kept walking, putting on my tough walk. I always walk fast, don't make eye contact, and never look scared. The walk is the way of exiting before someone figures you out. If that happens, it can be hazardous. You exhale, exasperatedly, and walk away with a 'yeah right' kind of attitude, making it seem like you can handle the situation but have someplace else to be. That impression usually works.

I guess he was too busy or wanted an easier conquest. He and I, we both moved on. Later, a man pulled up in his car. Since you are on the passenger side, they usually role down the passenger side window. This allows quick conversation, with the cops being none the wiser. Only, the cops usually know what's going on. If they choose to bust you, you might be able dodge the hooker van, which is a police van that picks up hookers.

When this car pulled up, I started with the basics and asked,

"You wanna go out?" He nodded, I got into the car. He started driving soon as I got in. I saw the handle to the door had been taken off on the inside, so the passenger could not get out. It seemed like a trap. I had to play calm, pretend that I didn't see it.

I started talking to him, trying to feel him out, but he did not answer. He started driving fast and reckless. I felt he was a psycho and he looked like he was trying to get out of the area quickly. I didn't know where he was taking me.

I went into fight-or-flight mode and noticed he made one mistake. He left the window on my side three-fourths open. It was an old-school window, with its roll knob still intact. When he stopped at a traffic light, I rolled the window down as fast as I could and sprang out, head first, landing on the pavement. That was one time it felt good to hit the cement. I figured while I might be sore the next day, he was gone.

Getting back to Frenchy, I had retired from being a car hopper and years had passed. I would watch other hookers and con artists at work, for what reason, I don't know. I think it was a distraction. I might have been judgmental, hoping to find someone who was beneath me, at least in my mind.

I saw Frenchy on a regular basis and was not attracted to him. Then again, sex was work, so getting horny was not one of my issues anyway. I was taking the C train home and saw Frenchy asleep, or nodding, which meant he might have been high on dope.

Since he got off the train one stop from mine, I followed him. It was after dark. He walked up a street in Harlem and disappeared between buildings, into an alley. I might have been crazy and bored but I didn't follow people into alleys at night. I decided to carry on with my business and went home.

I must have been crazy to be fascinated with that shithead. The next day, I walked past the alley and noticed it was an abandoned lot with junk cars. Guess who was sleeping in one of the car's front seat? Frenchy. I saw his matted dreads all over the glass. I felt happy – I had some ammunition.

Later that day, I saw him in Midtown and knowingly said, "Hey dude, I happened to be walking through our neighborhood and saw you in your studio apartment – you know, the one with the full window view." His fake French persona pretty much disappeared. He mumbled saying he just went there to get high and must have fallen asleep.

I had watched him rip people off and felt I would not stoop as low as him. I wondered why I could not be confident and cocky. Why could I not take pride in being a 'hustler', which seemed to be everyone else's mindset? Reality was he made more money than me, and I hated working the street. The anxiety was overwhelming, owing to which I was not good at it.

When he sneered and asked, "What's up hoe that can't get paid?" he struck a nerve. Being a failure at being a failure was too much for me to deal with, but that was how I really felt.

12.
What Name Are You Using? (1985)

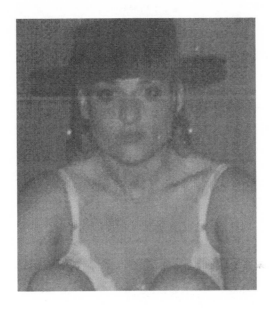

"What name are you using?" I was asked over the phone. "Uh, Jolie," I responded. Jolie was a female who I thought had the perfect life. She was gorgeous and had the toughest guy in the neighborhood as her boyfriend.

When growing up, I studied people, hoping I could polish up my act. I watched old movies with gangsters and was fascinated with toughness, thinking I would never get hurt again. Yes, it was naive, but it was all about perception. Mine was probably warped in some ways.

"Okay, Jolene. Make sure you're there at 9 o'clock. Look for a grey Firebird with Jersey license plates. If you're not there by 9:15, the driver leaves," she said. She would later be referred to as 'the phone girl'. I had just entered the world of escort services. I was nervous, so I didn't correct her as far as the name. I felt completely out of my element.

Until then, I was a bike messenger living in a house of a family friend, in Staten Island. It was a wonderful family, but it wasn't my family. It wasn't my home and I was at a point when I looked at life as a race that I was losing.

I was going to Staten Island Community College, taking glory in studying psychology, trying to be the expert even though I didn't have a clue. I had gotten my GED failing the first time. Now that I had it, nobody could call me a high school dropout. Yeah, I was moving move up ladder, so to speak.

I was a college student. Owing to the pride my father felt, he gave me a car, a blue 4-door Lincoln. It wasn't even his. It belonged to his girl friend; she had money. I guess she made the donation. It was strange he gave me that car. As a child, when I went to private school on a scholarship, one of my closest friends was picked up by a chauffeur in a silver Continental.

They were three sisters, and I had originally been a friend of the middle child. Then I got left back, ending up in class with the youngest. I learned to make and change friends quickly throughout my whole life because it seemed to change drastically all the time.

When I got left back, the younger one became my best friend. I would go to their pretty house, look at their pretty things, and think of how safe they felt. They didn't fight when they ate dinner and they actually had desert. They were rich, they were blonde and they had a beautiful mother who was friendly.

I liked being at my friends' houses because it was better than being home. The problem was I always felt inferior due to not having what they did. I would try to be good at sports and act like a clown. I had old clothes and rode a bus to school. I had a key to a home I didn't like. I always lost the key – not on purpose but out of habit. Losing bus passes and constant stress added to my woes.

I started cutting myself at the age of seven. This was around the time my mother was diagnosed with multiple sclerosis. All of a sudden, everything changed. To tell you the truth, I don't remember most of my childhood; maybe due to head injuries and drugs that followed. In any case, there weren't many happy memories.

When I started writing this memoir, I intended to hurt all the people who, I felt, hurt me. It was almost my primary driving force. Maybe that is why I never finished it – I was not stable or ready.

Now, I have healed considerably. I have more insight and self-awareness. I am going to be vague when it comes to my family because they are not the story. The story is based on self-empowerment and self-growth in the face of adversity. Let me get back to the situation at hand.

I was going to college, living my family's friends, then, bang, I was a call girl. Did it simply mean I was a high class prostitute? I didn't think I would be pretty enough to be a call girl because I thought I had to look like a model. Someone had talked me into trying, saying I was just the right age (19), and that with my hair dyed blonde, I could make thousands.

The phone girl had asked me if I did 'black men'. It seemed like a funny question. I found out later it was a real problem because even pimps asked their hoes not to do black men. So what if the pimps themselves were black? The reasoning was they could get robbed. Stick with the 'easy white dudes' who could be manipulated, was how it worked.

They asked me if I did bi-scenes and I just said yes, to everything else as well. This way, I didn't have to explain anything. I didn't know what we were talking about for most part. Once done with the phone call, I ran to the store and bought some cheap get-blond-quick bleach. Not much later, I became an expert in cutting and dying my own hair. For then, it was all about improvisations. Fake it till you make it.

How I felt was this. I was going to have money, which meant I was going to have power, quite like all the people who used their power against me when I was growing up. I would never feel helpless and inferior again.

It's like jumping from a height that scares you. Ideally, you don't think, but just jump. I had to try and pretend I felt pretty and sexy – that was going to be hard. Later that night, I followed instructions and took the ferry to Manhattan. A stream of thoughts was racing through my mind.

Did I look fat? Would they find out I was a fake blonde? What if they felt I was ugly? What if I didn't know what I was doing? The questions refused to go away. Finally, the ferry docked and I made my way through the cold, to a corner where I looked for the described car.

I didn't see it. I thought, maybe they found out I was not very pretty, or maybe they changed their mind. All of a sudden, a Firebird pulled up in front of me, with two men in the front. One asked, "You Jolene?" I answered with a simple "Yes." They told me to get in the car.

The driver introduced himself as Big Joe. The man sitting in the passenger seat was referred to as Uncle Vinnie. They told me we were going to pick up a second girl. A bachelor party was to follow.

We picked up the second female and she said hello. She told me to make sure I used my thumbs so I asked her, "What are you talking about?" She suggested that when we did the bi-scene at the bachelor's party, I should use my thumbs over the vaginal area. Her opinion was that men were easy to fool and wouldn't know the difference. I got to thinking if I had to do a bi-scene because I was not gay.

I quickly learned that this businesses gets you do lots of things that don't apply to what you used to do or who you used to be. I had just started a relationship with this driver and his sidekick, who sold coke to us on a regular basis. It was a norm I adopted and I became a regular bachelor party girl.

Within a month, I dropped out of school. I went to get my nails and hair done regularly. I even had a boyfriend, at whose house I would stay most of the time. He taught me how to freebase. I was making a lot of money. He was more than happy to assist me in using drugs at my expense.

I would let him use my car at night because Big Joe would come to Staten Island to pick me up – it worked quite like a door-to-door service. My new boyfriend kept telling me that the car needed fixing in some way or the other. Sometimes it was a new fan belt, at other times, something else. Since his father was a mechanic, he knew how to fix it. All I had to do was leave him money while I went to work. Wasn't that sweet?

In actuality, he was getting high for free all day and wanted money to get high all night. While he kept saying the car needed work, I was busy and didn't see the writing on the wall. After getting delivered to men like a pizza for a while, I realized I was getting played. I just left him, the car and Staten Island, moving to Brooklyn.

I spent years couch surfing and didn't feel like a bum. I always had money and paid my way around. The money well eventually runs dry. Then, you don't have money to pay for the lie you are living.

13.
Healthy Goodbyes (2015)

My therapist made sure I was aware that time was coming. We were ending treatment because it was taking place in a crisis center, funded only for a limited period. Besides, my therapist had his own dreams. Life was taking him to California.

I have been in and out of therapy since I was seven years old. Talking and walking out the door had become commonplace in my life. When you're a prostitute you might not have an admirable job and walking down the street of loneliness is quite the norm.

In the past, I had tried to buy and make people my hostage, in whatever way I could. This was new. I had no hostage and no drugs to run to. I was losing what I would have considered a sounding board or captive audience until not very long back. I had grown to feel I had a support system and a friend in that therapist.

I'd known him for two and a half years, since the time I was on interferon and was seeing dead animals on the street – only to realize it was garbage. Unlike the present treatment for Hepatitis C, the older method could well be a stimulant for a mental disorder. It was also very painful for many, me included.

There was no guarantee it would work but I had decided to

choose my battles. Instead of fighting strangers and hostages, I was going to fight a disease. I was running on ego fumes, telling myself I was a soldier who had to face demons; and geez, there were in the plentiful.

I would watch my shadow on the street and always feel someone or something might be behind me. Hey, I lived in NYC and was a hooker. Thinking about possible ambushes was not at all strange to me. Reality also was I suffered from undiagnosed PTSD back then. I felt mental health providers in the past were playing a game, like clue or scrabble. How else could they pop up with different diagnosis all the time? Depression, psychotic depression, bipolar – can I get a vowel?

Fuck! I needed help and the entire specialist business never seemed to offer any special insight. My mother suffered from anxiety. While mine might have partially been due to genetics, trauma in my life had become commonplace, so much so that no specific incidents stood out anymore.

The first time I went there I learnt it was a Crime Victims Treatment Center. I figured I was not worthy of help and the people there wouldn't like me. They would see I had two violent felonies and I was a hooker with HIV. I almost talked myself out of going, but then, I was desperate.

I walked in, met my interviewer, and started rambling. I remember going, "Like, um, I know I am, um, not considered a, um, I am a felon and I have violent felonies, but, um, ah." He cut me off and said, "Tell me about your childhood." After I gave him a brief summary, he said, "I think we can help you."

I felt someone lifted a weight, which seemed like a ton, off my shoulders. I could finally breathe. Someone thought I deserved help, as a victim, which nobody ever seemed to notice. Being the black sheep of the family is one thing. When nobody seems to see the part they played in the damage, it's more than infuriating, it's like beyond words.

Street life teaches you to always wear a mask and never show weakness. Although some play the victim, for most part I feel people don't know how to get real help and turn to drugs instead.

When I was going to Borough of Manhattan Community College, I took a course on people with disabilities. Among other things, it taught us how to be politically correct in how one labels and names people with disabilities. When I learned about what happened at Willow Brook State School in Staten Island, it made me angry, sad and scared. It was re-confirmation that society was far from perfect. Sometimes, though, it seemed perfectly evil.

Why did I torture myself   by making my major 'Human Services'? I guess it was because that's all I knew and I was definitely not the chemist type. I also was learning about life and myself in the process.

It is hard, sometimes, to look at situations objectively. In my case, I personalized almost everything other than being a mother because I had no children. One of my triggers was an abusive and neglectful mother because I had not made sense of my childhood yet.

I believe that to heal and grow you have to have a healthy navigation system. I went from cutting myself to chronic masturbation to eating and binging. At one point, I realized I could use my negative energy externally, after which I started vandalizing and fighting. Did any of these coping mechanisms work? No. However, they functioned as seemingly effective   distractions from my inner madness.

Lack of power you feel in life when it comes to hierarchies, social navigations, behaviors and expectations can make you resort to bravado and overkill. You can, for instance, start hating your surroundings, and then, categorizing. Your mother was dominating, so you don't like dominant women; you have been a subject of racism, so you become racist.

I strongly believe that one reason the majority rules is for a brief moment it gives almost everyone an illusion of unity and safety.

Getting back to the situation at hand – it was my first experience with a 'healthy goodbye'. Before then, I did not think there was anything healthy about separation. It was about hate, abuse or neglect, and not to forget, abandonment.

When I had first started treatment, it was based on six-month intense psychotherapy. It had been extended for an extra two years in my case, because of the considerable progress I was making. I was audio taped sometimes. Since I wanted attention badly, I was like, "Hell yeah! You can tape record anything." Those tapes became my own keepsake afterwards. Listening to oneself in hindsight can be very enlightening.

The first therapist had been an intern. Right away, I was ready to ramble and rumble. It was like I felt that everything was competition, and I had to over talk and control the atmosphere completely. Instead of him being like the typical therapists from my past who either nodded their heads or told me my time was up, this guy said, "Can you stop talking?"

Oh my God! That was something I hadn't planned for. "Of course I can, if I choose," I responded, and continued to say,

"Isn't that what you're here for, to listen to me? I would think I was making your job easy." He explained I was using sarcasm, stories and humor as a way not to feel. That made no sense to me. When he challenged me to stop talking and sit in silence, I felt like I was going to jump out of my skin.

To me, it was a competition and I could not let him win. I had to pretend I could do it without any problem. I was obviously discombobulated. He told me when I talked about trauma I had been through, it was like I was talking about someone else, like I was telling a story, almost scripted.

I felt uncomfortable in a whole new way. I had never felt that way before. I had exposed myself to him and to myself. "Holy shit, he's right," I thought. I was talking for no real reason and I was not present. Stories I told were true. Some were horrific. However, I felt I had to use shock for him to hear me. He challenged me in a nice way. He asked me to go home and dared me to turn off Facebook, the TV and my phone, and just lay there. I was to tell him how long I managed the next time we met.

What a challenge. I was not backing down. I went and did what he suggested. Lying on the floor – I'd been sleeping on it for eight months because of back problems – I realized I didn't know how to breathe. I didn't know how to relax. I would have rather fought a whole block than felt that way at that moment. It was something I knew I had to face and change. The journey began.

I would go see him as he recorded our sessions and I would try to learn to be present and quiet, in theory. I would look at him and try to figure our connection. He was attractive, a new type of attractive. He was not a thug and was very smart. It was a whole new world for me. I did not know about healthy relationships. Right away, I had to see him as a possible mate, date or rejection. I had lived by extremes for too long. I did not know everything was not based on sex, money and violence.

Eventually, I was able to see him as a guide in my life. Then, he finished his internship and left. Again, I felt feelings of abandonment coming back. However, I had to remember everyone was not codependent like me. I had to realize life went on. I had to be happy of strides I was taking.

To have caring relationships, I had to learn what caring was. When people are lonely, some get cats, dogs or other pets. It serves as no more than a distraction or a substitute for what people really desire. The animals are used and discarded when no longer needed. I did not want to be like that.

I knew I had to stop looking for hostages and distractions because they could easily be mistaken for happiness. I had to learn to love and like myself.

The first guy who interviewed me when I got there took over my therapy. In the beginning, I was trying to find out what was wrong with him because I was comparing him to the previous therapist. Very quickly, I developed a less challenging and more supportive relationship with him.

One day, he told me he knew I was going through changes. Since my computer broke down and someone had donated one to the center, he was offering to give it to me. Initially, I was not touched. I was getting a handout. On the other hand, he heard me. I was about to get my associate degree and my computer went kaput right before finals. I didn't know how to get one and

I was not resorting to old ways to make money.

I felt like a kid on a Christmas morning. Until then, I usually tried to buy people and loyalty. There, I was learning it was okay to take as well. I left with the big tabletop computer. While I was leaving, security stopped me and made me prove how I got it. I had to call my therapist and have him come down to the lobby. What if he was mad at me? What if he got in trouble?

He came down and verified the situation. I was embarrassed. I felt bad for putting him through that situation. I felt he wasn't going to like me anymore and he wasn't going to be nice. I became an obstacle, or so I thought.

He walked me outside. As I looked for a cab, he asked, "Are you okay?" He didn't hate me. He was worried the treatment I'd just received might have disturbed me. "I'm fine," I said. I really was. The security chap's belittling left aside, I found someone who was there to support me. I could do my schoolwork to boot. I was more than fine. I was ecstatic.

We had done a countdown for six months, to prepare for our separation. Although I was trying to be adult about it, I was scared. I was not going to be in treatment there anymore either, because my time had expired. I tried to crack a joke, but could only manage with, "Are you on social media, like LinkedIn?" I was trying to establish a way to stay connected. He said he was not going to stay in touch with me via Facebook or any other social media platform, because that was not the way our connection was supposed to go.

I wanted to get mad and ask, "All this time, you just pretended to care?" Reality was he had gotten a job in California and was moving. His life was continuing and mine had to as well. "Why can't we share phone numbers?" I was thinking to myself. I wouldn't bother him; I just didn't want to be left alone to face the rest of my life.

My life had improved. I had fished the Hepatitis C treatment so I was not as unbalanced. The pain in my back had gotten better and I started sleeping on a bed. I was in Hunter College, studying for my bachelor's degree. I had left my enabler's house after 15 years. Life had grown and changed. I had new ground to cover and the change seemed scary as hell.

When we shook hands and separated, I walked away quickly. I went and sat in Morningside Park and cried because I felt alone again. I had the ability to see it was a 'healthy' separation and not abandonment. I truly cared about both therapists who had worked with me. While they had different approaches, both were on point. They blessed me with their knowledge and support.

I realized I was happy for both because their lives were evolving, like mine. They had their own challenges. I remain glad I walked into that center for therapy, specifically with my trauma, because it turned my life around.

14.
S.H.U (2001)

A sergeant escorted me into the building. I had been out of isolation for only about three weeks. The officer working there said, "Hey, I remember you," as she took a picture of me, like how they take mug shots. I had a minor injury on my face. I think someone scratched me with tweezers or something similar.

There's one thing that sucks about being Irish. When someone slaps you, your injuries can look like a train hit you, which is because of pigmentation. I wasn't even thinking about the consequences of my behavior because I was mad that I got an injury. It'd be a shame if someone thought I got my ass kicked.

Why was I in the S.H.U (special housing unit)? It involved me assaulting an officer because I did not want to stop fighting. If I got injured in a fight, I had to make sure the other person's injuries were worse.

I went into the cell, sat on the bed, and looked around. In some ways, I like being by myself. That way, I don't have to watch my back. Besides, I don't have to be around a bunch of loud annoying women who talk in stereophonic sound.

There is only one drawback to wanting solitude in prison. Bitches can't shut up anywhere. As soon as you feel relaxed, like you might go to sleep, someone yells to somebody through the windows. "Yo yum yum, dumdum, yaya, yoyo, crunchy, munchy," and a whole bunch of other corny names come flying out.

You can try to block out the noise, but it's impossible. There is always one major player in the windows who thinks she is the window thoroughbred. All they usually talk about is their fly gear and their ghetto- fabulous (ghttofab) life on the street. You get tempted to blow a hole in their story. You can tell, just by listening to them, that they ain't shit.

Then, there are followers who will always be someone's cheer-leader and keep saying things such as, "Yeah, yup, for real, for sure and that's real." Typically, they never have anything to share on their own.

I was an angry individual. Most things bothered me. This included graffiti I saw in the cell, which was not in abundance, because we didn't have handles on our toothbrushes or real pens. When I saw things like "jojo loves smo smo" carved on the bed frame, my initial reaction would always be, "Why don't you learn to love your kids first?"

The authorities gave SHU inmate's pieces of soap. I never understood that one. A book cart would go around, no more than once a day, with books that had probably been sitting on it for more than a decade.

The facility was building a new S.H.U for women who, they felt, were more secure. During its construction, instead on having our one-hour out of the cell in a single cage, they allowed recreation with up to three women at a time.

When I noticed the drop ceilings, I wondered if one could go to another area by crawling. Then again, I was not into   doing chin-ups at the time. It would take a lot of upper body strength to get on the toilet and hoist myself up.

Don't get me wrong, I wasn't trying to escape. For some reason, I always feel like I have to figure out everything in advance to protect myself. For instance, I wanted to learn how to pick locks, in case someone ever held me prisoner. I knew I was a prisoner then, but I could deal with lawful imprisonment because at least I was safe (or so I thought).

I always knew some inmates got pregnant and some others got beat up. For most part, women who were not sexually active were not forced, and then, there were others who were hyper-sexual. I guess it's a behavior that one adapts to. I could never understand how some women had husbands and kids visiting them, then had dikes at work, and then, would flirt with male officers.

At the time, I was a hater. I didn't know how to 'live and let live'. For the first six weeks, they did not allow me to mingle with any other inmates. It was because, technically speaking, I had assaulted staff. I had to have a sergeant and two officers handcuff me to take me to a shower. Although it seemed crazy, it made me feel important.

It's a hard life, when you live in the ghetto and want to feel safe. You want others to leave you alone, and you want someone to know you exist. I guess it was too much to ask for. I had become detached from human bonding because I hated the world, and everyone in it.

I didn't believe people when they said something nice, and I took insults seriously. My entire existence felt miserable. If I thought I met inmates who shared some of my outlooks or any kind of common ground, I would have soft spots for them.

I noticed that by telling everybody I was HIV positive, it made some people get close to me. We shared something more important than a cigarette or a favorite rapper. We shared a stigmatized illness and the struggle that came with it. While it was the number one killer of young black women at that time, and more than half on the inside were HIV positive, denial and throwing insults was commonplace.

I had my own style to keep idiots at bay. I would say, "Don't worry, I got what I got, but I ain't gay. Even if I was, it wouldn't be your bed I would slide into anyway." I had an array of defense mechanism jokes ready for them. One was, "I just talked to my STDs and they said you don't have to worry because even they don't want your ugly ass."

I know I should have been more shameful. However, I felt being in prison was a time to let my hair down. I was no longer a prostitute hiding my status. That had killed me for very long and I felt like a dirt bag. What other inmates thought about me was nothing compared to how bad I felt about myself.

Nobody challenged me on the subject until this one day I will never forget. After about six months, I got so sick of the noise, I decided to become a part of it. If you can join them, beat them at their own game, I figured. I had established my mouth. An inmate asked me, "Do you read the bible?" I answered, "Nah, not really," and added that I could not understand it.

"You know you're going to hell, right?" she asked. "Well, I guess I'll see when I get there," I said sarcastically, and laughed. I always found it annoying when people who had terrible character, verbally abusive and what not, thought that they could get a free pass to heaven by simply reading the Bible, that Jesus would fix everything.

I figured religion to be a crock that essentially scared and brainwashed people. A demon seed telling me I was going to hell was almost funny, but not quite. A few days later, a new inmate was moving into the cell that was across from mine. I recognized her voice right away and thought, "Oh, fuck, her comes mighty mouth." It seemed like a threat to my comfort zone.

I went to my window and told those in the surrounding cells not to believe a fucking thing this boasting shit head said. All of a sudden, the Bible sales woman inmate yelled, "Say it to her face." I was stuck because she was instigating an argument between the new inmate and me. Since she put me in a spot, I had to save face. I simply said she did not have what it would take to do anything anyway.

I had no real reason to hate this woman. When you are a control freak and see others that are controlling in nature, I guess it kicks your shit up. The new inmate and I coexisted but the shit starter was still trying to get me going. She never went to recreation. She would sit safely in her cell and throw peoples' crimes in their faces, like if you were a supposed baby killer, she'd rant about it. I don't think she had any real knowledge of anyone, but she was vicious with her words.

They kept us locked in our cells 23 hours a day. After some time in the S.H.U, I was able to go to recreation with other women, and they put us in sets of no more than three. That way, chances of you running into a fight remain slim, but they do happen.

That night, she started reading her bible out loud. I don't

mean aloud, but loud. She continued to thank God that she did not have the 'monster' (AIDS), and that her pussy was pollution-free. I could not believe she was using the Bible to harass me. She went on and on. Finally, I said, "You better thank God you're alive because someone is going to kill your ass one day."

She did this every day for a month. By then, she lost her audience and nobody even talked to her. She had burnt her bridges. A new inmate came into the cell next to mine. She sounded white and talked a lot of shit, but I found her amusing. I kind of liked her style because there weren't too many white chicks capable of standing up for themselves as far as streetwise ways went.

When I started getting used to her voice, a correctional officer who I had had numerous run-ins with got into it with her. I couldn't understand why this officer seemed to be looking for a fight. I found out later. An officer who had thrown me on the mess hall floor during my first visit to the S.H.U had gotten eight months paid leave. When officers hear stuff like that, they would like the same.

If you don't get much mail, and if you have no money in your account, I believe it increases the probability of you being a victim of police brutality. At times, they do pick their targets.

I heard the officer talking shit, as usual. This new white woman, whose name I never learned, said, "Bitch, I will spit on you." The officer unlocked the cell, went in, fought with her and pulled a pin. What I heard next was the sound of   boots running down the hall. Then, the men with boots arrived.

While she was in the cell next to me, I could almost feel what was going on through the wall. I asked the inmate across from her, "What are they doing to her?" She told me the inmate was on the ground, getting kicked in the face and head. I heard one of the male officers say, "Oh, you're trying to bite me?" Again, I felt the violence through the wall. Eventually, the noise stopped.

They took her out of the cell with a blanket over her head, probably to hide her injuries. I was dumbstruck as I saw her walk by without a single cry. I always wanted to look and act tough. However, that was a surreal moment because it reminded me of how quickly life could change.

We never saw her again. I heard they pressed charges on her for assaulting the female officer. I felt like part of me died. Even though I didn't know her name, I felt like I shared something with her, something I would never forget. What pained me was I couldn't do a fucking thing to help her.

One day, about a month before I completed my time in S.H.U, the Bible inmate blurted out through the window, "McCarthy, do you know why I hate you?" I called her by her name and said, "Damn, you're still alive" No one had heard from her in a while, which was certainly not normal. Then, to answer her question, I said, "I don't know, hmm, because I'm white?" She said, "No, it's because I'm sick too, and I don't know how to talk about it."

Just like the surreal moment where that woman got beat up by officers, this moved me for a second too. My thoughts of how I could try and find a way to get into the drop ceiling and climb into her cell so I could drown her in the toilet finally vanished, as did my anger. I understood her better, and how could I not? I hated a lot of people for no apparent reason. It was probably because of things I wasn't ready to face yet.

15.
First Attempt, 2004

"Is the whole world full of shit?" It was a typical question I asked myself when I came home from prison the first time. I thought as soon as I got out the gate and got away from the loud boisterous women, I was going to be okay.

When I arrived in Port Authority, it felt like a swarm of bugs running into and over each other. I felt out of synch because I usually avoided crowds, and not because I wasn't imprisoned with others looking up my ass and talking like they were yelling all day. This time around, it was a bunch of robots racing each other in the train station.

I was away for only three and a half years. Upon my return, I noticed everyone was staring at their phones and talking, which I quickly learnt was the new fashion statement. Walking and talking to someone using hands free, looking like you escaped from an insane asylum.

When I heard I needed a metro card, I had no clue what they were talking about. When I left, they used tokens. I went to the machine and was getting an anxiety attack. I felt someone was going to say something because I was slowing progress, and I would react. I tried to rush and stuck the dollar in, waiting for the card to come. Eventually, someone helped me.

I got involved with a hospital I frequented in Midtown and went through the basics as far as HIV care and follow up go. They were sending me up the block to a specialist ear nose and throat doctor. I didn't feel the need to go but I was trying to stay busy. I was clean and I was trying to do everything responsible.

I wasn't even in the office five minutes, and he said, "You know you had a broken nose." I was like, duh, and said, "Yeah, I know, I was there when it happened." He said I needed to get it fixed. I told him I already got it crunched back into place. He got a little aggressive, saying my septum was deviated. He showed me how one nostril looked bigger than the other.

He said, "You told me you like to exercise, so don't you want to breathe better?" I guess that was what I needed to hear. I was never good at breathing because of my anxiety. I thought it might be my nose that was responsible. I said okay.

He then jumped in with, "I will also give you a nose job for a thousand, under the table, because Medicaid pays for the anesthesia, which costs the most." Who asked him for a nose job? Dude had a lot of nerve and was acting like an addict trying to sell a stolen bicycle – all impatient.

I was ashamed I didn't have a thousand. I told him, "Well I got a big chin too. If you take away my nose, my chin will be lonely." He seemed disappointed and said we still needed to do the surgery on my septum. He scheduled it for almost the same week.

I also went to the HIV clinic and talked to a counselor. He said he would teach me how to use a computer and asked me for my email address. Next thing I knew, he was making sexual advances. Was he serious, in an HIV clinic? I thought I had weird taste. Not to mention, he was married. I eventually left because I didn't know how to set boundaries. I ran to another place.

A doctor who was very professional there was the one who worked in the emergency room (ER) the night my nose was broken. At that time, I had been on methadone. Whenever I had an episode, I went to the familiar places for help. There I was, at my methadone program, hours after getting my nose fixed. I kept telling myself I was going to get painkillers and it was going to be okay.

The on-call doctor at the ER was talking with me. Without warning, he crunched my nose back in place. "Hey! Why didn't you tell me and warm me first?" I asked. He pointed out that if he did, I would move, and then, it would not have worked as well. He also said he had seen me before. I told him it was my regular hospital, thinking I would get brownie points. Then, I was waiting for the script.

He came back with an icepack and a Motrin 800 and said, "Sorry miss, you are not getting high for free tonight." Although professionals can be blunt, I respected his position. Not at that moment, of course.

Getting back to Dr. Desperado – I followed through with surgery to have my septum fixed, which was an extremely painful experience. I still cannot believe I was so lost I let someone put me under, digging in my face. When I woke up, I found myself on a journey with no directions of what to do about a pain so intense.

I cried like a baby and called my boyfriend of the time to say I was hurting. I told him I was by myself and didn't know what to do. That boyfriend was about as sensitive as a vulture or hyena. However, like I've said, my anxiety and low self esteem had resulted in me keeping very bad company.

I felt damaged. Which normal guy would want me once he knew my story? As a result, I tried to find someone who I thought would appreciate me and couldn't judge me. That approach was a disaster in the making.

What strikes me is these supposed professionals should have ethics, right? If not, why am I labeled by society and they are the pillars of community? This kind of approach from a professional was not an isolated incident. As a matter of fact, I have had many professionals and supposed mentors show me how unprofessional and unethical they can get.

Once, someone put me on to a 'dirty doctor' who would write scripts for Xanax. After I left, I hit the closest pharmacy, because I was in Brooklyn and didn't know the area. I handed the pharmacist the prescription and he immediately asked, "Do you take HIV meds?" I was like, what the fuck? I got very defensive and asked, "Why? Do I look sick? Why the fuck should you care?"

He responded calmly. I guess it wasn't hard to see I was a drug addict. He said if I gave him my HIV pills, he would give me my Xanax for free. At the time, it sounded too good to be true. Back then, I didn't get or take HIV meds. I felt I was not going to be a guinea pig for the next generation. My philosophy was, if I didn't get instant gratification, like false euphoria from a drug, I was not bothered. Who gave a shit about the future?

I assumed it might be a stake out by the cops because they knew people on methadone programs and drug addicts were a sure bust, sooner or later. I said, "Nah, just give me my pills."

Then, I walked out to kill some time, till the prescription was ready. I was not familiar with the neighborhood and it was cold as hell. I figured it was a good time to shoot a bag of dope, but I had to find a safe spot to do it.

After walking a few blocks I found a pizzeria. I went in and asked if I could use the bathroom. They said it was for only for customers. I debated buying some pizza and came to the conclusion that food was not a priority. I walked around the corner and saw an alley with a dumpster as well as backdoors to the pizza place and other stores. It seemed like a perfect place to get straight or at least neutral, to fight withdrawal. Hopefully, I could get a little high as well.

Heroin is a full time commitment. The price of feeling safe, carefree and comfortable comes back to collect full restitution, with interest. I was trying to block myself from the wind and partial snow. In a doorway, I got my works set up, which I had gotten down to a science. In my mind, I was the master of ceremony.

I shot up and quickly put my contraband away, while I waited for the comfortable numbness to take hold of my body. The outcome was disappointing. I had bought the dope from an 'unknown' and it was whack (not good). However, it was part of the game and it at least made me feel I would not be sick from withdrawal for a while.

I lit a cigarette and looked at my surroundings. Suddenly, my attention went towards the dumpster. I thought I saw movement. I hate seeing stray animals suffer and still love them enough to try and befriend and feed them. As I looked at the dumpster, I saw a pair of feet sticking out. I thought someone had dumped a body there. It didn't shake me much, and I just kept smoking. Then, I saw one of the legs move. I thought whoever it was could still be alive.

While the dumping of a body did not rattle me, when I thought that someone was trying to live, I had to get to the rescue. I walked up and asked, "Hey, are you okay?" I moved some of the garbage to see what I was getting into. What I saw was a black man, upside down, almost at the bottom, with a lot of garbage and scraps around. He said, "Yeah, I'm just looking for food; they be throwing out lots of good stuff if you catch it at the right time."

My heart sank. I saw him resurface as if it was his norm, with a piece of bread that was not even clean. He started chewing it as he climbed out. Until then, I had tried to numb myself from life's pain and suffering with drugs and disassociation.

Sometimes, life catches you off guard. If you have forgotten how to feel, someone else's misery brings you back to earth with a crash. I had come to hate the world because I felt it hated me. However, loneliness is a bitch when you try to act like a robot on drugs.

He was actually in a better mood than me. Even though I was a terrible listener, being self absorbed and all, this homeless man's happy-go-lucky persona was charming. He was happy despite the fact that he led an obviously destitute life.

I gave him a cigarette, which is always an icebreaker. I guess it's the same as people with supposed better culture, which brings out glasses to share wine. I ran back to the pizzeria and decided if there was a time to buy pizza, it was then.

The homeless guy I met was a Vietnam vet. He told me about

things that mesmerized me. I was almost sad to finally get up from sitting on some boards in the alley and say goodbye. People are not born in dumpsters. At one time, he was a soldier. It was something to be proud of. Then, he was a nomad who ate out of garbage and still had better attitude than me.

At that stage of my life, I was grateful to meet anybody who was nice and did not try to hurt, play or rob me. This guy was interesting to boot. Wow, what a day.

My point is this – there are some beautiful people who lose their socialization skills and isolate themselves from others. Even though they are in full view for you to judge or scorn at, you have no idea what brought them there.

16.
Pleasantville

As we drove into Pleasantville Cottage School, I made a mental note that there was no barbed wire on the fence and that the gate was left open for cars to come and go. A long road led to a big house, which they called a cottage. It made sense, since they called it a cottage school.

I was introduced to my cottage parents. They explained the rules and informed me that since I was 13 years old I was allowed to smoke. You have to remember, this was way back in 1979. While I didn't smoke, a lot of the other girls were watching, so I said, "Yeah, I smoke." I went outside and hugged my father, then watched him drive away in his girlfriend's VW bug.

I met the welcoming committee, which seemed friendly. We went to the porch and one of them gave me a cigarette. I tried to smoke and look cool without choking. Immediately, I was asked if I knew G talk. "Huh, what's that?" I asked right away. Soon, I started learning how to talk in a code language.

The first three months went without incident. My cottage was the youngest out of the three female cottages. There were several male cottages too. One day, I saw a kid having an episode, who school authorities were taking to a building. I asked the other kids, "Where they going?" They told me that it was to the isolation building, where they put kids on a drug called Thorazine.

At that time, I was terrified of what I thought might happen in isolation. When they have you on a sedative, you could be tortured. I had no idea then that constant sedation would become my goal in life at some point in the future.

I decided to run away. Maybe I was looking for a reason. I ran down the long entrance and knew I had to do it fast, before a car came and saw me. If I had to climb over something, it didn't matter. It was like I was in the "The Outsiders" or some other movie about tough kids who were rebels. I felt like a female version of "The Fonz."

It was fun to use imagination, since my hand tremors were a dead give away to other kids. I felt I had been thrown away and forgotten. My parents didn't tell me it was a home for emotionally disturbed children when they took me there. I knew my dad cared about me, which is why it was bothersome. Why would he let me be there? Why didn't anyone want me? I was soon to learn the power of negative attention.

Running away, I made my way to the Metro North train station and hid in the train's bathroom. I didn't have any money or I would hitchhike. My problem was I had nowhere to go. I called a friend and she gave me the number of a girl who lived in the Village.

We bonded instantly and I lived with her for a few weeks. I called my dad regularly and he begged for me to tell him where I was. Finally I gave in. Like countless times before, he drove me back to Pleasantville.

My mother had signed over my custody to the state after the injury she received during our scuffle. I don't know why   she

Had custody to begin with because she seemed to hate being a mother. She was sick from multiple sclerosis. I was seven when it happened and it was very hard to understand why she was so unstable.

When you're a child, you can't understand why everything is unpleasant. I felt I was too big to bully, so they disowned me.

My dad finally got a new girlfriend named Jill. He met her at a church where he worked as a super. The last time I ran away, she let me move into her beautiful apartment. My mother finally took back custody, because she knew I would run away again. I think she was also worried when I hitchhiked from upstate, being only 13 years old.

Jill was a special woman. She treated me like her own daughter right away. She had three sons and the oldest was my age. The other two were a little younger. She lived in a wealthy building, which had separate elevators for maids and servants in the past.

The apartment had vacant space. I stayed behind the dining area, in what seemed like a small apartment. "This is what being rich feels like," I thought. My father had a way with women. He always picked women who were established financially, or at least responsible. He would work doing private contracting Here and there as well.

Eventually, we all moved to the Hamptons. She paid for the house. My father and I were able to live there all year round, while she and her sons left after the summer ended. It was a dream come true – just me and my dad. Sometimes, what you wish for doesn't turn out to be what you thought.

His girlfriend had paid for me to go to a catholic school down the road. I would go there during the day but a majority of students lived there. There was one more teenager, who, like me, was not residential. She was blond, rich and, believe it or not, a bully. She was a little taller than me, athletic. She was real pain in the ass that made me uncomfortable.

My father was not home most of the time, so I was in the house by myself. I was scared of the trees and the quietness of the country. One night, when he came home, I said, "There is someone at school who is picking on me – I might have to punch that someone in the nose." To my surprise, he said, "Don't punch her in the nose; punch the back of her head through the front."

He must have been drinking because he was not the violent kind. I could see he was not happy with the arrangement. The next day, I waited for her usual routine and held my breath. I didn't even look her in the eye when I punched her with all my force. Next thing I knew, they expelled me for breaking her nose.

Again, I was the 'bad kid' who failed in life's norms. I felt I had learned the most valuable lesson of all – never let anyone pick on you because you don't have to be a victim. This mindset gave me a false sense of empowerment. It turned out to be a recipe for disaster.

17.
Identity Crisis (2014)

How dare you question my beliefs or perceptions? Do you realize I base my identity on what I feel, which is hate and bitterness? Trivializing that is like dissecting one of my limbs. While I don't have much in this world, you will never take away my insecurities, hatred or feelings of bitterness. That's what keeps me going.

I know that midlife crisis is kind of part of the parcel, because life might not feel satisfying. Maybe you're simply trying to regain your youth, or maybe it comes from wanting to get laid and feel attractive again. Due to multiple sexual experiences, which included several traumatic ones, getting poked was not my idea of happiness. It did not make me feel special. As a matter of fact, it made me feel used.

Once, I tried to have a relationship with an attractive looking guy. When he spoke, I knew he had a dark side. Who was I to judge or be picky? He was HIV positive, which I felt, was a beginning.

Half way during our first sexual encounter, I had a flashback and started fighting him. I was telling him I wasn't scared of him and put my knee in his chest, lying on my back. He got up and told me to leave. What could I say? Even I didn't understand what happened. I didn't have sex for orgasms because they didn't happen anyway. However, I wanted to feel connected to someone.

All my relationships have been toxic in some form or the other. For once, I decided to stay solo. When I was ready to leave, I visited my old faithful closet, one I had in someone else's home for over 15 years. I looked at my choices of clothing. My tough guy clothes were on one side, and the old hooker gear, on the other.

I did not want to wear either. I had spent thousands of dollars on drugs and had never treated myself too much. No vacations or shopping sprees. My clothes told a story in themselves. You can have all the brands you want. Mine were old and had little other than bad memories attached to them. I knew I had to change everything. Part of it was living by within my means, which meant without much.

I realized that most considered poor people as lazy or a strain on the economy I felt I might as well learn to live with my current status and use it to grow. Instead of living off someone's couch, I decided to pack my stuff and go to a shelter. It was not as bad as I imagined, but it had some major challenges.

It was a shelter for felons – men and women who wanted to reintegrate into society. There were people there who had done anywhere from a year to 44 years in prison. It was interesting talking to my peers. I saw most of us were still trying to live on ego fumes about who we were. I wasn't a gangster, but you couldn't tell me anything because I wasn't listening.

There, I met an Irish guy who had done over 30 years. At first, something drew me to him as a person I wanted to know. I always wanted a brother who would have taught me the ropes. I guess this guy was a substitute. We laughed. I tried to show him modern technology, but he was not open to change.

Cutting a long story short, we did not get along for long. He was a control freak, just like me. I also noticed he was racist and homophobic. While I have bitterness over some events with blacks, I also have trauma associated with whites and Hispanics. Everything was not black and white anymore, especially because I was starting to learn and open my mind.

He told me I was a traitor and I felt he was implying I wasn't using my whiteness to good effect. Then, our relationship dissolved. He was not a bad guy, just not ready to change, and he liked thinking he was in control. He soon died an untimely death, owing to an overdose. While we had our differences, he still holds a place in my heart.

I had finally finished the entire course of Hepatitis C injections and the treatment was successful. It felt good because I had kicked a disease's ass. It was a new war story. Even though I was an intravenous drug user in the past, I decided to fight for my life instead of fighting to kill myself. Part of the treatment, which was comparable to chemo, was injecting some medicine every week. It made me feel like I got beat up and aged 20 years overnight.

I was never the type who did something for the future. I slept on the floor instead on my luxurious couch for a whole year. The disease was beat and it was time for my next challenge, finishing school.

I walked into the class on the first day of a new semester at Hunter College after finishing my associate's degree at another school and saw the front row empty. I assumed my position there. That way, I would not be overlooked or unheard. I was a little more defensive and insecure than usual. It was a class based on Ethnic Study, which was part of my curriculum. To get my degree, I assumed I would have to hear about how much white people sucked.

As the class started filling, a black woman with a strong presence decided to sit right next to me. My social anxiety started growing. She was not only large and all on my elbow, she was black. It was one of my triggers. Anytime I saw a black woman with a strong presence, I assumed we are going to bump heads.

I have a thing about women, period. They hurt me in my past, as a child, emotionally and physically. White women who should have been my guardians when I was growing up used money as leverage. They also used it as a weapon. When I was in the ghetto, dealing with angry black women and men, I believed Women were more pissed because they had misplaced anger.

The class proceeded for a week or so, by which time I put my guard down a bit. Then, sure enough, my neighbor blurted out, "Everyone is black, and if they don't know that, they're stupid." I felt it was amongst the dumbest thing I had ever heard. Once I put my defense system in check, I tried to make sense of the conversation. If I went in for the attack, I wanted to obliterate her, because I took her statement as a challenge.

The statement she made was a little harsh. Only, she was a smart woman and had logic. I learned her statement was based on genealogically. Her point was all of us stemmed from Africa, and it was the origin of mankind. This might sound crazy – soon as I saw the point, I was relieved it was not a hostile statement. It seemed fair enough to me, and why not? Where did we come from? Nobody can really prove shit, so why not Africa?

In the past, I thought it was a little strange, how Jesus was always white. Since I wasn't religious, it never really made a difference. The difference between the past and that moment was I was in college and not jail. I no longer had to worry about mob mentality. Even though I felt uncomfortable listening to some topics, I could finally imagine how blacks must have felt listening to white versions of their existence.

Eventually the teacher said, "Racism also affects white people." I was like, halleluiah, yes! I felt my feelings mattered and couldn't wait to elaborate about my struggles of being the only white person on the block. To my dismay, it was not time for me to speak of my pain and suffering. The teacher went on to say that since white people had lost their hold or superiority, they were, more or less, suffering from identity crisis.

I was like, are you fuckin' serious? I had to remind myself I was in college, and to excel, I could not be throwing tantrums. I got a tummy ache and ate some more food from the vending machine, to distract my train of thought. I was not able to see the point the teacher made. I felt like a little kid, cheated out of my ice cream cone.

Over time, my neighbor and I became friendly. It is much nicer to come to school to learn and feel respect for each other, than to feel angry or insecure. I needed to focus those fears on passing tests, and not in trying to prove the fragility of my ego.

After I left school one night, I walked up to 68th Street and Madison Avenue, to catch a bus that would take me home. There were a lot of grand looking buildings that I thought were for foreign diplomats. It was an expensive neighborhood. Madison Avenue had many stores with beautiful window displays. There was little traffic as far as customers went. How the stores managed paying rent, I thought to myself. Even if they charged a million bucks for a hat, how did they keep up the stores in between?

For someone who never had assets or stocks of any kind, money is very simple to me. I either have it or I don't. I looked at all the beautiful buildings. Although people seemed a little snooty, WASP like, the area offered an element of safety. In other words, if you go into a chic overpriced coffee and cookie shop, the only fear you have is not being able to afford the price.

"Someday, I am going to live in my own home and have a safe place to go," I thought, as I looked up to the windows. My father had been the super of a building that was attached to a church on 74th Street and Madison Avenue. I walked up to it and stared at the window where his office used to be, on the ground floor.

At one point, my dad had tried hard to be a good father. He came to pick me and one of my friends up from school every day. He would drive us to his workplace, where we could use recreational facilities, such as the pool. My father made a lot of mistakes. I found out he fabricated my last name. He was married to more than one woman and was not able to face his past for some reason. He had a friendly way and made me feel cared for most of the time.

When I was there, I met someone who worked in the building. He told me the pool was closed, and that it was filled with cement. To me, it simply showed how life moves on and does not wait for your cue.

I remember walking up to the building and saying aloud, "Hey dad, remember that school you used to drive by and say I should go there one day? Well, I go there now. I don't do drugs anymore. I know a little more about myself and am learning balance."

I walked to the next bus stop and waited for the bus. While it felt lonely, I was finally facing my fears. I realized that in order to get some balance, I could not afford another doomed relationship to distract me. I needed to learn to love, like and appreciate my life. I got on the bus and headed towards my new residence, the shelter for felons.

I had given up my 15 years rent-free ride on someone's couch and realized I had to change and face life if I wanted to grow. Damn! It was one hell of a way to go because I shared a room with a paranoid schizophrenic. I told the staff she was unstable and I was unable to sleep. They said she was not dangerous. I told them we both had violent histories and were nuts, asking them to do the math.

I started to see the whole nonprofit title for a business as very misleading. If you get paid to provide services, how can you call yourself a nonprofit organization? It makes it sound like they do it out of the kindness of their hearts, as philanthropists. To me, there is nothing wrong with an honest approach. Just tell the truth – you are keeping jobs and grants to help certain populations, and one hand washes the other.

I would rather have someone tell me I was in a shitty position as far as having no foundation. That can be changed with A, B and C. If there is a genuine agenda to help people grow, baby steps are understandable. When someone talks to you like you are nobody and says you can get kicked out of a shelter, it's rough.

I noticed there was many people who did wrong things, including drugs, multiple times, and were always welcomed back. My being HIV/ PTSD positive sucks. However, it is also supposed to be a way to get special services. I was there for a year, going to college, working, and with clean urine. Despite that, I got no assistance. My main problem with the system was this. They got extra money for someone like me. It almost seemed like they wanted to keep me there, and not help me grow.

18.
Bing Monster (1999)

"Look mommy, I'm good at something – being a loser," I thought to myself. I had just started adjusting to my surroundings in the dorm. I actually liked the person sleeping next to me, which was not the norm. All of a sudden, I heard my name yelled from the officers' station. I got up to find out what they wanted.

I was hoping to learn it was time for methadone, or that someone was bailing me out. The officer told me to, "Pack up." This is usually a good sign because you might be going home. She was rushing me, telling me to roll all my shit up into   my blanket, "since you ain't got nothin' anyway." I hadn't acquired much because I had not been in for long. I did as instructed and threw the sack over my shoulder, like Huckleberry Finn.

I bid my goodbyes to those I liked and those I thought might care, which made it a quick exit. "So, where am I going?" I asked her. She didn't really reply, like it was a game, or like I wasn't important enough to address. We stopped in front of building 12 and she said, "You are going to the Bing for 14 days."

"What for?" I asked. She dismissed me saying she was an escort, not a lawyer, adding that I plead my case with someone else. She cracked a few jokes with the Bing's main officers and made her exit. The new 'Charles in Charge' kept rushing me. She was talking to the other officer stationed there, ignoring me like I was an animal, unable to communicate.

A different guard escorted me to my new cell. As I entered the bottom tier, it got eerily quiet. I knew all eyes were on me. Not because I was special, but because I was a newcomer. The eyes were assessing me.

In the Bing, an inmate worked as a suicide prevention aide (SPA). I usually can't stand them because I have had incidents with them. If they see you wearing gold, they come like sharks, smiling and asking you if you want to sell. It could be your ring, chain or anything they can exploit.

I guess I hated them because I was an addict, which meant I sold out quick, even for a pack of Newport. I had sold my jewelry several times until then. Working as SPAs, they tend to act more like professional con artists.

I heard someone scream through a door, "Who that?" A voice behind another door replied, "I don't know, some white g i r l."

Then, the noise started again, yelling back and forth, trying to get attention. I guess inmates look at noise as amusement. However, it becomes extremely annoying when you are kicking a habit and trying to sleep.

I walked into the cell, noticing it was just like the cells in any other building. Only, the door had a slot in it, through which the authorities could pass food on a tray. I heard the door slam behind me. The SPA looked through the window, and then walked away with the officer like a puppy.

I figured it was best that I try and get comfortable. My hands were starting to shake increasingly. In the morning, I would get my methadone. For then, it was just a waiting game.

Dope fiends lead typically crazy lives. You want the numbness. You put yourself through hell, thinking that that, sooner or later, you will be comfortably numb. Will life have meaning then? Can you hear me laugh? Inside, I felt I was dying.

With regular and unrestricted access to heroin, I might choose to stay in a cell for the rest of my life. I always wondered if drug cartels needed a guinea pig to test their heroin. What about the holier-than-thou police that needs to establish potency of drugs, so as to broadcast it on the news?

I will be your drug tester. However, I come at a price. I want a comfortable bed and a TV. The latter, in case I want to do something while awake. Plus, no roaches – I have a phobia. Seems like a fair deal. Wow! That sounds heavenly; having an intravenous drip of opiates. I will never commit suicide because I do not wish to take a chance with punishment coming my way in the afterlife. Besides, nobody might care if I die. Fuck that! I am not going to make it that easy for them.

"Do you want to take a shower?" I heard through my door, as the slot opened. I could see the officer and the SPA standing, with their two big heads blocking the view from the window. I answered in the negative and said I needed to get my methadone. That was my priority. I heard a snicker from the SPA, while the officer muttered something about people not even wanting to wash their asses. The slot closed.

The Bing in Rikers Island is jail inside a jail, consisting of an isolation-housing unit. My crime in 'criminal land' was punching a plastic window in the medical center, which was part of a tantrum I threw. The windowpane cracked. They charged me with destruction of state property and gave me two weeks in the Central Punitive Segregation Unit, also known as the Bing.

My mention of methadone was ignored. They were messing with me because I would probably deal with any other violation of my rights in a better way when compared to them taking away my only coping device. If there was a button on the wall that said, 'To die painlessly, press here,' I might have done it. At that time, I would much rather have dealt with the Gods of Wrath.

The torment of being physically confined is a piece of cake in comparison to your inner demons having a party at your expense. My body ached and my shaky old hands were back. It made me feel helpless, like a scared child. With my mask stripped away, I felt dorky, sickly, needy and vulnerable.

Anyone taking my drugs away was a fear worse than death. I hated the world and had to feel again. Issuing of methadone was the reason I punched the window in the first place. I had just gotten to Rikers. By the time you get through 'central booking' and in, it can take up to 72 hours. In admissions, you are going cold turkey. The anticipation of getting methadone is excruciating, almost like you are drowning and are in need of air.

I was about to get medicated at the window, when there an alarm went off. We were forced to face the wall, while a bunch of correctional officers ran by with sticks, shields and helmets. We were moved to a particular section of the building, with that annoying alarm still at it, like an air raid siren in old war movies. All movement had been put on hold. The anxiety in my head, mixed with withdrawal, made me feel I was about to have a seizure. Tick tock, tick tock.

A black woman in the area started asking me about my jewelry. I said, "I didn't get my methadone, so I'm not in the mood." That was her cue to start ranting about how she, "don't back down to no white bitch," that she didn't give a fuck about my methadone, and what not. I just got up and punched a window, with my body shaking all over. That's how the story went.

There I was, once again, my methadone hung over my head – The story of my glamorous life. That night, I counted bricks in the wall and just stared at my cell. I was glad we could control our light switches. I will not turn off my light for anyone. I am scared of the dark and feel my surroundings should be visible at all times. I tried to masturbate to make the stress go away, but I couldn't do it for shit. I felt ugly and awkward.

The next day, I finally heard someone yell "methadone" in the corridor. Many women were like, "Me, Yo, cell 5," "Yo, cell 28," and "Don't forget about me." Some cells had jokers. I hear someone yell, "Go get your jungle juice." It was not the first time I heard that, it would not be the last. While you hear a lot of shit, such people are not important until you get 'straight'. Straight is when you're no longer withdrawing. You are functional, you feel stable, and then, you can figure out whose ass you want to kick.

The officer came to my cell and asked, "You get methadone?" I went, "Yes!!" and almost jumped off my bed as she opened the slot, telling me to put my hands through. I was handcuffed through the door. With my hands cuffed, I was let out. Other inmates on methadone were assembling against the wall.

We walked down the hallway in general population to get our methadone. Our handcuffs were placed in front, enabling us to drink our methadone at the window. If I wasn't feeling sick and clumsy, I might have basked in the negative attention.

Inmates from the general population stared at us. They were told not to talk to us, like we were all so important. Being a part of the Bing Monsters had boosted my damaged ego. I was as real as it got – a complete fuck up – they had better recognize my extremities.

It was like playing a part in a movie. Only, all I wanted right then was to drink that orange liquid from a cup, which would make my pain go away. I got to the window and watched everyone ahead of me get their methadone. Part of me was screaming inside. Shut up, hurry up and drink. Cop and go mother fuckers – this is a saying on the street, meaning keep it moving because you are drawing police attention to the spot.

When I got to the window, my hands could barely hold the cup. I drank it and felt like life had new meaning. While methadone takes about 20 minutes to take effect, I knew instinctively that I was safe. I felt I could breathe.

When withdrawing, my body slows down. While withdrawal is essentially physical, the mental state is a significant factor. Since addicts are used to 'not' feeling and 'not' thinking, the reality of living life on life's terms can have quite a catastrophic effect. Once straight, I decided to take a shower. I was walked to the shower area, in cuffs again. When I saw the shower, I could not

help but laugh. They could not be serious. I had to take a shower in a cage? The shower had a set of bars that locked in place, and the officer watched whoever was showering the whole time. It felt like a scene straight out of Silence of the Lambs.

Some women were arguing as I walked back to my cell. I heard one saying real loud, "Bitch, that's why you don't get mail. When was the last time anyone visited you?" The other one said, "You a bum bitch and you live in that 'House in Virginia' anyway." I was thinking to myself why living in a house in Virginia would be ammunition? I found out later it was a code for HIV.

When I returned to my cell, the fact that I was in jail for attempted murder hit me like a brick. I didn't have a clue of what happened. To add to the nightmare, I kicked an undercover officer in the groin after getting out on bail. I was facing two violent felonies.

It felt like a dream, with my imaginary audience watching. Was I in a movie or some altered reality? Life could not be this, I thought. I had to handle it, not that I had a choice.

When you have a felony and are going to prison, you have to be free of methadone. This is because it is not part of medication they offer inmates who move from city jails to state prisons. Consequently, they have an accelerated detoxification program, where your dosage reduces on a rapid schedule.

There was no more comfortably numb. However, getting straight was better than nothing. It was cold and I still needed air. I continued feeling hot and cold intermittently, owing to withdrawal. I was glad I was by myself but the noises never stopped. If it wasn't women yelling about how much they loved and missed each other, it was how someone ain't shit and how someone would fuck someone else up when they came face-to-face.

The luxury cell comes with an all-in-one toilet/sink. If you're lucky, there is enough water pressure for you to brush your teeth. You have to press a button, as is the case in parks, with water coming out of a little fountain. That, there, was far from a park, and the button looked nasty as hell. I would kick the button for the toilet to flush because I did not want to touch it.

I heard seagulls singing, which got me to think of what might have happened to my dogs after I got arrested. I missed them and was scared about their safety. My boyfriend knew I was in trouble with the law but he didn't expect me to get arrested for another felony. He was probably caught off guard.

I remember the last time I saw him. We fought because he said I was a crack head. I was vicious too, calling him a part-time faggot on the train. The name came about because of his history, working as a male hustler, before I met him.

With him, I had tried to be mother-figure of sorts. He had no one since he was 13, no parents, brothers or sisters. He lived on the street after running away from group homes. We had met coping for dope, in line, with everyone pushing and shoving. I remember talking shit, which was not new, saying, "Yo, I am disabled, so stop jumping the line."

He challenged me, asking, "What is wrong with you?" I said, "I got AIDS bitch," to which he quickly retorted, "You do? I do too." Instantly, there was a connection. The only problem with my new AIDS soul mate was that he was a pothead, and not to ambitious.

I thought I could control him by being the breadwinner. I was living a double-life, selling myself to buy a comfort zone with someone. I got to a point where I started resenting him, mainly because, truth to told, I needed help.

I came home one day and saw a phone bill for over $600. This was on account of him lying around all day, ordering on demand wrestling for $59.99, at my expense. I had a plan for him.

The next day, after getting off work at the escort service, I was dropped in front of my methadone program, as was usually the case. I had to sit there for two hours, till it opened. I frequently saw a man on the program also waiting, as I did that day. I went up and asked him, "Why are you so early?" He responded, "I am not early, I slept here." That was my cue, someone needed saving. I heard how he was a Vietnam Vet and lived on the street. I suggested he could stay with my boyfriend and me in Bronx.

I took him out for breakfast. After we got medicated, I brought him back to the apartment. My boyfriend was probably at his methadone program because he was not home. I got the homeless man to take a shower. After he did, I cut his hair and had him put on my clean clothes.

My boyfriend came home and asked what was going on. When I explained that the nice older man needed a place to stay because it was cold outside, he was livid. He said that the man was a "charity case," to which I responded, "So are you."

My dogs had chewed up the cushion for the futon. The homeless man had started putting his stuff down on the floor to sleep when I said, "No, don't sleep on the floor." I even let my dogs sleep on the bed if they want, so I asked my boyfriend to, "Move over and let him lie down."

He said he was not sleeping with a homeless man breathing on his face. I said, "Just move over and let him in." I felt it was the right thing to do, plus, it seemed like some kind of power play.

The ironic part was the guy decided to go back to the street. He said we were too out of control. Before he left, he helped me sharpen my knife, which I carried for self-defense.

I had gotten jumped a few nights before. Since this guy was a war veteran I thought he would know the real deal about protecting oneself. As a result, we talked about combat strategy. I didn't realize I was going to see a man that night, and that everything was going to go left. The knife would be part of the evidence they had against me.

Coming from being a 'control freak' due to a fear of others having an upper hand into a situation like that was reality that seemed too surreal. Well, I sure didn't feel like a boss then. Besides, in reality, I never was.

The next week involved punching and kicking my door because of not getting my methadone on some days. The reason was most of the women that were on it had left, and the officers didn't want to go through the whole process for just me.

Once, my hands and wrist swelled up. I gained experience in being a nuisance. In some time, I realized that the large bucket under my bed was better to make noise when compared to banging the door, and it was pain free.

The authorities obviously did not care, but I had to feel like I was not invisible. This is one of the main problems with people like me. The whole concept of control and fighting authority, with the 'I will show them' mindset, is a perfect recipe for disaster and self-sabotage.

19.
Growing Pains (2016)

When I was on interferon, I hated everybody. I saw dead animals on the street, only to realize I was looking at garbage bags. It felt like I was being tortured. The physical pain from past injuries was immense. However, interferon purposely inflames joints. Sounds crazy? Well, it puts your body on high alert, getting it to think it's under attack. Then, the soldier (white) cells go into overdrive.

Don't get me wrong. Physical pain is exactly why it's called a pain in the ass, neck, back, and shoulder or wherever else it decides to erupt. However, mental and emotional turmoil is my Achilles heel. I have never felt safe in this world from as far back as I remember. When I was a kid, what I saw most in this world was pain. It felt like an accident waiting to happen.

I remember very little about my childhood but I do remember trying to prepare myself for doomsday, when everyone was going to turn on each other. Maybe that's why I am such a Walking Dead fan. I guess we seem to be fascinated with our thoughts of despair.

I still frequently tie my closet shut because any blind spot keeps me on edge. What do I do to combat these thoughts? I watch paranormal witness shows so I can see how others have dealt with ghosts and ghouls. I know it sounds ridiculous.

Getting back to the old treatment for Hepatitis C – it was rough. I felt I could get nowhere with my shoulder, neck and back because doctors were not taking it seriously. Finally, when they were going to do surgery, my insurance wouldn't cover it. I hoped for relief and wanted the situation to improve by any means.

On this one occasion, I sat in Harlem, watching buildings being built everywhere because of gentrification. I saw an old building and felt bad for the dirty old bricks that were not being cleaned. The old buildings were just deteriorating. I felt I was going through something similar. Talk about focusing on and obsessing about negatives.

I did not go back to drugs, but companionship, or the lack of it, was still difficult for me to comprehend. Eventually, I met a man in recovery, who was a character. I figured I was one too, so we could bounce wit off each other. I usually don't date men who aren't HIV positive. With him, I think I knew it wouldn't amount to much. I took it as a friendship for most part.

When we finally kissed, I thought I was going to choke on his tongue. I went, "Damn! Why are you so are aggressive? How did my breakfast taste? You should know, with your tongue in my stomach."

Right away, power plays started. He said, "Why should I change the way I kiss? because you don't like it?" I thought to myself, "Umm, maybe, dumb ass." That, there, was a warning sign; we couldn't even enjoy a kiss.

Later, after his arrest, I visited him upstate for three and a half years. I must have done that because I wanted to feel needed. In my mind, I was just doing the basics, like visiting once a month and sending minimal funds. His time away gave me time to concentrate on school and work. It was one way to feel I had a significant other without much risk.

When the date of his release got close, he whined about not having a place to go, nothing to wear and what not. He said he was going to be stuck waiting for parole because he was homeless. Although we did not have any sexual chemistry, I figured, "Fuck it." I felt I was probably being nervous because of my PTSD.

Unfortunately, I was used to going an extra mile for people because, subconsciously, I felt I had to. When he was to leave prison, I got a hotel room and bought him clothes to wear. I asked myself if I really wanted to sleep with him. Did I really need to spend money? The clincher was he never showed up.

He never called and went back to his old routine. I saw him about three months later, walking on 125th Street, with a woman. I walked up and said, "Hey, happy birthday." His birthday was five days before mine and we always talked about the zodiac sign we shared. We were both Taureans.

He told me the woman with him was just a classmate and I shook hands with her. I had no bad energy towards her. Whatever their relationship, she could have it. I wasn't even mad at him. By then, I knew that's how he operated.

I feel when you chase someone, it's not because you miss the person, per se. It's the feeling of abandonment that makes you try and fix things.

My experience with him turned out fine. Some problems solve themselves. Ours was a relationship of convenience. We used each other. I got a college degree and he got a few candy bars. I could cut my losses and keep it moving.

Just like being scared of the dark and watching horror movies about evil doings, I realize you get what you ask for. Why would you pursue a partner or friend where the energy is uncomfortable from the start? Learned behavior is a factor. Women who served as examples for me when I was growing up had power because they were breadwinners.

I guess I might have been looking for a man like my dad who would cater to me, because he had no foundation. Anything was possible. I felt I did not have my father or a home because of the fact that he depended on women. As a result, I wanted to be the boss as well. Only, I just got used a whole lot.

On a brighter note, there are good things that stood out in my past. These included me going to a gym where I would take my anger out at a heavy bag as well as get some attention. My ego needed to feel I was tough because I felt insecure. Thinking you have to plan for doomsday and trying to learn how to punch better than predators is a lot of bad energy. That's what made me tick.

Once, I walked in the gym, when, from far away, I saw a woman hitting the heavy bag. I noticed she was not hitting it correctly. While I have dibbled and dabbed in a few styles of martial arts, I am not a master of anything.

Right away, I had to go assess the competition. I walked over, saying to myself, "She doesn't even know how to punch, she's slapping the bag." To her credit, she was slapping the hundred pound bag with enough force to make it dance. As I got close, I saw she was using her core, and doing combination, to boot. I got closer and noticed she was missing a majority of her fingers. She could not make a fist even if she wanted.

My insecurity flew out of the window. I was fascinated with this woman who was doing her thing despite her disadvantages.

We started talking. I found out she had a life that made mine look simple in comparison. She did not tell me about her life as a war story. However, she was open and honest. What struck me most was she was happy. Unlike me, she didn't hate the world.

Instead of wanting to find fault in her, I was trying to bond. When we were leaving the gym, I offered her a cigarette. She smiled and said, "No, my body is my temple. Why would I hurt it?" I was dumbstruck. Who thought like that?

For the first time, I could not bond with someone over a negative, which was my norm. Until then, I bonded with people because we did the same drug, or hated the same people or were misfits trying to take pride in our weirdness. There was something different with this woman. We remained cordial in the gym and never got close. She still touched my life because she loved and valued herself. It was new to me.

When I worked with dogs at the animal shelter, I didn't know how to say nice things, even though the animals were my life. I probably would have jumped in front of a car to save them. However, when I addressed them, I would say things like, "Come here dumb ass," and "Stop that, stupid," in a soft and playful or affectionate manner.

I didn't know how to express caring sentiments or I felt it might have sounded corny. I think I can count the number of times I heard the word 'love' while growing up on my fingers. My mother was responsible as far as my health went. She would also advocate for me if she thought an institution was harming me in any way. I feel that came from her responsible side. She had been an activist and it seemed like she enjoyed being mad and uniting with others through those channels.

When I would write to her from prison, she would send the letters back, grammar corrected, saying I sounded illiterate. One might say it was helpful in correcting my spellings, but what was with signing her name at the bottom of the letter? No "Love" or even "From." It was like I was a business associate. No. Even they get a "Sincerely yours." Sometimes, she would just write "Mom" at the bottom.

I know that's not a crime. The distant feeling, however, set the stage for our relationship in my formative years. The only time we got close was when we fought. Then, it got very personal. At one time, I was nervous to talk around adults. I was told children should be seen and not heard, while my dad and his girlfriend drank before driving. His girlfriend was a professor at NYU. There were feelings of inferiority – intellectually and financially.

Hey, I was just a kid. Once I started acting up, it was a case of overkill. Nobody could shut me up. If you were mean, I would chew you up and spit you out. It seemed fit to be a rebel and I didn't realize I needed balance in life to succeed. People like me, who feel invisible or inferior, tend to walk and talk hard. Without security, life felt very unstable.

My father joked with me when I was a child. After I got HIV, I was living with a stranger who I met on the street. My father would intervene sometimes and try to take me to detox centers. The strange part was, while he was much friendlier than my mother, we never had an honest talk about anything.

Quite a few years back, I had played detective. I went through his Merchant Marine trunk and found phone numbers. I called all of them. I learnt his name was not real and I had another half brother in Louisiana. He never told me about where he was from or any other details about his life.

One day, I tried to shock him into reacting, and said, "Guess what dad, I am a call girl. I won't have to be on the street." He just looked straight and didn't say anything. Now, I feel bad about that because it must have hurt him. At the time, I felt hurt by my family as well.

When he passed away, I was on methadone. He died in another state so I could not travel. When my brothers took his ashes back to Ireland, to be buried next to his mother in Belfast, I would have loved to be a part of the journey. I wanted to learn about his past and his family but my drugs came first. It is very shaming when you see what precedence addiction played in your life.

I am sober now. I will go to Belfast eventually. I think I'll get some kind of closure at my father's gravesite.

Now, I laugh at the fact that when I went to Rikers in 2009, they put me in a heat sensitive building. I am not heat sensitive but it didn't matter to them. I was freezing my ass off, lying on my stomach, with my arms uncomfortably pinned under, trying to stay warm. I was also listening to a small see-through Walkman that we could buy in Rikers.

A song came on and I felt it was my national anthem. It was One Republics' "It's too late to apologize." I would sing it and think I was going to get my satisfaction when all of it was over.

My partner of five years, who was no more than a 'get high partner', would try to apologize and I would make him squirm. The funny part was he was never planning to apologize. In some ways, I guess we like to torture ourselves – giving people so much power and such an important role in our lives when the connection is not even real to begin with. That way, you can lose what you never had.

Now, I see addicts are usually in codependent relationships. Most wouldn't know what a healthy and happy relationship looked like even if it hit them in the head. We don't have a healthy comparison to go with. That was my story, at least.

There were several other negative incidents that involved other people, which I don't want to revisit. I want my life to progress. I don't want to go to war or open a Pandora's Box.

I could not avoid racism because it was a factor in my life. At some point, I saw I had issues with it. You cannot tell a story without the whole truth when it concerns rights and wrongs of institutions and society, or without admitting your own exposures and biases.

20.
Solitude

It was quiet. While it was boring, I was grateful to get a break from the mayhem. I was going to the quarantine section of the Bedford Hills Correctional Facility for Women, a maximum-security prison. They were not equipped to deal with much out of the ordinary where I had been sent to do my time, which is why I was in the max facility, temporarily. Sometimes, I think women doing hard time are easier to get along with than ones doing skid bids, like myself.

From the safety of a window, I studied women passing by underneath, as I looked down on all the hardcore felons. "Hmmm," I thought, "I know that asshole," "Oh, hell no, she's back?" "Hey, I know that idiot." It was amazing I never saw anyone I liked. Maybe it was because I was not a happy camper and I didn't like anyone – for most part.

I didn't trust people. Every time I tried to test waters, I got the same results. I didn't want to think I was loved or that I had friends. That way, I would not be disappointed.

There were two doors to go through to get into my room. The wall facing the hallway was all glass. They could see everything if they chose. Luckily, I was left alone much of the time. After a while, you get used to the degradation. In Rikers, they get you to strip, squat and cough, while you bounce, which is a lot of fun – and it feels even better if you are detoxing and can't even walk properly.

Once you get to prison, they have you strip down and take everything out of your mouth, like a denture or partial dentures. I'm not going to lie – it feels ugly. To have to stick your tongue out so they can see you don't have anything hidden in your mouth is crazy. Worst part is when you have to bend over and spread the cheeks of your ass while someone looks at your privates from the rear.

I could never understand why they wanted to look at our assholes when we had an easier hole to use. Reality is they make you spread everything so much, they can see both.

At meal time, someone would come in dressed like a beekeeper suited up, slide a tray in, and shut the door fast. I didn't mind, at least not consciously. However short our interaction; I felt my presence was acknowledged. Even if it was fear of catching something, at least I was not invisible. My life had amounted to this. "Well here comes a nurse; that will be enough social stimuli for a while."

After about a week, they gave me an old TV with a VCR, and three old 8-track tapes. One was 'Bambi', which was not my scene. Then, there was Ice Cube's 'Next Friday', which was great. It was funny and the sound track was something I could dance to while I exercised. I also had the 'X-Files' movie, which I watched about 25 times. Then, it got to be too much.

I found a book called Ghost Soldiers under my hospital bed. At first, I was like, "Oh, geez, a G.I. Joe story." Having limited options, I read it. It turned out to be a great book, based on

WW2 and how POWs were treated. They were shipped around much. At times, they had to drink their own to remain hydrated. That made me snap out of my 'woe is me' mood. It made me

realize that when it comes to life feeling like shit, and in my opinion, over rated, I was not special. Many had been through worse.

At some point, a doctor came in and checked my skin. She said she thought I was getting better, but would not confirm what the problem was. Talk about bullshit. At least the itching was gone, which was my main objective. If they wanted to play dumb, what choice did I have? I didn't know anything about scabies until about three months ago. Inmates simply discussed it as a maybe.

An inmate had asked for help and said something was wrong with her skin. However, the staff and other inmates either ignored her or made fun of her. Since I am HIV positive and have dealt with stigmas my whole life, I don't like when people pick on easy targets. I continued to talk, walk and touch hands with the inmate during the closing of our prayer meetings.

Next thing I knew, it felt like a bug just scurried through my underwear. The feeling is so sudden; you tend to go right to the area in question and scratch. I was scratching everywhere and the inmate I caught it from had gone home. There were a few others who were complaining about itching and bumpy skin. However, when we reported sick, they said it had nothing to do with each other. Medical said we all had our own health issues and it was not something contagious.

Not much earlier, I had gone to an HIV doctor and gotten my HIV meds changed because of taking AZT, effects of which were unknown to me until then. AZT is a very strong HIV med that is not used widely anymore because of known side effects. The pigment in my face had changed and it looked like I had bleach thrown on certain areas. When I found out it was from AZT, I was angry nobody let me know.

When you've been an addict for decades, you miss out on a lot of information and what's happening in the world; maybe even a family that cares about you. When you realize you don't even know what you're taking for HIV, it makes you feel stupid. Who can I blame, though? Who would listen? I knew I took my life as a joke, and I was paying the price.

I was waking up with blood on my sheets, from scratching at night. When I complained, an officer said, "If you keep your area clean, maybe you won't have bugs biting you." Instead of the women sticking together, they tried to figure out who brought it in. Who gives a fuck where it came from? Whatever we had, we had. Who gives a shit as long as we get rid of it?

When she was still there, the original woman with the symptoms got picked on, but I didn't get in on that shit. Soon, I noticed I was becoming the new scapegoat. Someone even accused me of washing my ass in a slop sink, which was kind of ironic. I had laughed at people who were accused of that in the past. Karma is a funny thing.

One day, in my mandated drug group, I got angry with another inmate. I told her I had too much on my plate and that she, "better leave me the fuck alone." I was asked to leave the group, and had to go clean the facility as a consequence.

I was in the recreation area of the prison cleaning, when some women asked me what I was doing. I started showing them my skin, telling them I was going crazy. One of them said to the others, "See, bitches be coming to jail and all of a sudden they care about shit, but they wasn't caring when they were on da street." I felt like putting my foot in her mouth. I also felt tired and overwhelmed. I hadn't had a good night's sleep in months.

On the inside, you can't forget where you are. The problem is women don't kill each other like men in prison, giving rise to a lot of false alarms – not good for the nervous system. One tactic I found very interesting was that instead of fighting, women would sometimes just be spiteful. If someone had dentures, someone else would flush them down a toilet while she was sleeping.

The first time I went to prison, a dentist asked me, "What the hell happened to your teeth?" It wasn't that they were messed up, because that's not uncommon. He said he could tell someone had spent money on my teeth at some point due to the caps and crowns. The question was what happened?

Someone hit me with a rock or brass knuckles about a month before my first felony. It was dark when it happened. I had acrylic nails. During the grappling, part of my nails ripped out, which hurt the most. Then, of course, there was the blow to the teeth.

I went to the NYU dental school the next day. I thought they were going to fix the damage because they had given me braces when I was 12 years old. I had pulled the train track braces off on my own after running away. Besides, my teeth had straightened by then, and I found a way to rip the braces off.

After the fight, I had cracked front teeth. The dentist told me there was damage to the nerves. It would take about $700 for every tooth I wanted to save. I went back to getting high and got into a fight with a guy in a bar who called me a transvestite.

He head-butted me and broke my nose. It was not a good time in my life.

There are some things I won't mention – things that made part of my life more traumatic than I'll ever be able to explain. If there is a time to do an overhaul, I feel prison can be it. If you got to get your teeth fixed and don't want to walk around looking like a Halloween pumpkin in your neighborhood, prison is the time to get down to business.

There is only one problem – they don't believe in saving teeth. Every so often, they get pulled. Then, in comes new furniture. I had no idea you would go to the dentist and he or she would extract one tooth at a time, with you still looking like shit. I told my dentist to go for broke and take the whole top out as soon as possible. I figured, why save three or four? My days as a glamour model were over.

I was a big mouth rebel and would argue with officers. When I got my top teeth pulled, they had a lot of jokes. While I would try and be a smartass, I couldn't talk because I had no top teeth. I could barely pronounce anything right.

I tried and eventually got my fancy prison denture. It even had my prison number on it. Talk about a brand name. That was my second time around in the land of correction. I got a partial and it had my new prison number. At that point, the inside of my mouth had two different state bid numbers, to stay with me forever. I felt like a sexy motherfucker with scabies and a handful of real teeth left. I put on the 'Next Friday' movie and danced to its soundtrack. I tried to feel better. Since I didn't feel sexy, I tried to break dance.

It felt like I was about to lose my mind. I wrote to   Albany and Grieved Medical and even called my mother, who is not a nurturer. When it comes to rights and health, though, she is on her job. She called the superintendent. Next thing, I was quarantined. They still did not admit there was an outbreak. What they did was put us on a pesticide type of crème for our skin, which we were to apply from the neck down. We had to leave it there for a while. It was like creaming yourself down with Raid, the bug killer.

I was over thinking my position as an Inmate Liaison Committee (ILC) representative. I was a supposed liaison between the superintendent and inmates in my dorm. The job was basically a crock. One of my responsibilities was making announcements to housing units, about what movie they would be watching next weekend and about delivery of sanitary napkins.

For some reason, I got anxious when making announcements to the residents of the dorm. I would go from one bed to the next, instead of making one speech. It was strange because I was a hyperactive talker. I usually have no problem letting all my business out. When it came time to reading from a script other than my own, I got camera shy. I couldn't do it with a straight face. It felt forced.

I think the reason it bothered me was I liked playing the clown. When you are a clown, it gives you an outlet. You never have to worry about rejection or failure because everything is funny or sarcastic. It makes you feel you have control. That is probably why I sucked at being an aggressive hooker, trying to milk it for all it was worth. When you try to sell yourself or haggle, you have to face more rejection. I did not like trying to oversell something that was embarrassing to begin with.

If I'm not mistaken, ILC positions started after the Attica Riots, which resulted in the loss of lives of several officers and inmates. It was a way to make inmates feel they were being listened to and supported.

Once, a woman told me she had a suggestion for Mother's Day that she wanted me to share with the superintendent. It was that mothers in prison should get gift baskets. I was dumbstruck. Instead of sending gifts to kids at home, it was about giving women on the inside gifts for Mother's Day. After all, they were mothers, so what if in jail.

I tried to bring the outbreak topic up in my surroundings. When I discussed it with other ILCs, they said it was not part of protocol. I should have known better. Listening to them was like asking a fish how to run.

My last time in prison, I had nine fights in three and a half years. This time around, I had none. The first time, I got many disciplinary tickets and lost out on my good time. The second time, I had no tickets. I felt I might get home on a merit date. However, I had my kicked ass in a whole new way.

I saw destruction of incarceration is deeper than conflicts with other inmates. It's a fact that you're at the mercy of the facility as far as mental and physical health go. The fact that inmates are made to feel less is painfully obvious.

I did not want to try and compete with other inmates the second time around, about who got more mail and who had more commissary. At the end of the day, I wanted to learn how to live in my own skin. I saw I had one hell of a job ahead of me.

21.
Painful Realizations

When I came home from prison, I remember I couldn't wait to eat pizza. Old habits die hard. I also couldn't wait to get hair dye. I wanted to go red again. Salt and pepper looks sexy on men, but I rarely find it appealing on women. I was hoping my body aches would disappear with the grays.

I had a laptop for over a decade. However, because of being computer illiterate, I would get frustrated and slam it shut, swearing it had a virus. I was home again, my hair was red again, and the pizza sucked. The question was, "what next?" Don't get me wrong. My ego felt it could squash people like bugs, but my spirit seemed broken, almost non-existent. I had been living off anger and frustration for long. Without it, I felt lost.

I might have gone back to old habits as far as changing my appearance, but I was not going to make the same mistakes again. I gave myself some rules that included, don't find boyfriends in a parole office or drugs program; don't get high; and change everything. The reason for having to change things was simple.

Even the music on my old iPod was DMX, asking everybody to suck his private parts, and Sysco crying about being incomplete after his boo left. I realized all my music was angry or sad. While I didn't relate to happy music, I found some to work with.

I would go to Narcotics Anonymous (NA) and Alcoholics Anonymous (AA) meetings regularly. Both made me sick. The group at NA seemed like a bunch of 13 stepping wanksters and AA attendees seemed like a bunch of cornballs. Finally, I had to admit I was not in a good place with myself. I stuck to the routine and looked forward, not sideways.

I remember instances of walking down the street and suddenly having anxiety attacks. I would start thinking I was about to get into a fight or was going to get attacked. I would have to imagine the street was a painting, and not real, to calm myself down. Whoever I thought was a threat probably didn't even know of my existence. I would force myself to keep walking, trying not to show any anxiety.

The more you think about it, the more disoriented and awkward you get. It's like when you trip and try to cover up after. I was not able to carry a weapon anymore, which might seem like a weird gripe. Until that time, though, I was not used to walking around empty handed. I knew I could not afford to get into a fight, especially with a weapon.

By then, I found out I had PTSD. I started feeling better simply because of the fact that it made sense. Once you know why you don't feel right, you can at least try and sort it out with logic, therapy and proper meds.

The world continued to feel overwhelming. I remember going to my regular hospital for everything, including yoga and acupuncture. I was fighting for life. I had to try anything that could lighten the load.

At the acupuncturist, I asked for help with my back. I would lie on a massage type table and get needles placed all over. Once they were in, my movement was restricted. The acupuncturist, Paul, would put on Indian music and turn the light off. I would lie there, staring at the floor through a hole, and swear someone or something was going to ambush me.

I didn't like having pins stuck in me. It felt like an attack. While Paul and I remain close friends till this day, I didn't trust him at first. I didn't trust anyone. He was friendly. Only, I wondered how someone could be friendly sticking a needle in my leg, with my foot getting a jolt of electricity.

He was very patient, considering the first time he put a needle in, I whined and complained. I remember going, "Ouch, why did you have to twist it? It was already in!" As he was walking out the door, he just smiled and winked. I asked, "How do you hurt me and wink?" "That is like a rapist leaving a thank you note!" He looked at me, dumbstruck. How could he respond to such a statement?

Next, I went to yoga class upstairs, where I swore the instructor was gay, simply because he was a gentle natured fellow. It turned out he was previously in the Special Operations Forces and was engaged to a woman. Obviously, my perspectives were limited.

When it came time to meditate, I sat Indian style. Everyone closed their eyes. I couldn't, because I don't like the dark. It makes me feel vulnerable. I watched everyone relaxing. When I did get around to closing my eyes, tears just started to pour. I don't know why that happened. It was very uncomfortable.

Seeing how hard it was for me to do the basics made me sad. I would walk into NA like I had a third leg. I'd sit like a dude and put that 'don't try to mess with me' face on. The following day, I would go to an AA meeting and tell my war stories, using shock value to feel I made an impact.

Since I started school, I spent all of my time working on myself. I put Spanish language translations all over my walls so I could learn. I wanted to grow and find out how to navigate this thing called life. I heard about Facebook and thought it was corny. In reality, technology challenged me. I was barely using a cell phone properly.

A lot of old timers and addicts who haven't been keeping up with the Joneses will shun modern technology. However, once we get the hang of it, we're like little kids with new toys. It's all about baby steps.

Going to college, I had to face my laptop. I opened it, slowly learning what social media was, and from there, it was game on. From that moment, I had a way to get the attention I craved without having to fight or face arrest.

I decided to stick with toilet humor on Facebook. It was harmless and not about race, religion or politics. The worst reaction I could get was, "That's gross." I was okay with that. To me, I made an impact and got a reaction. It was validation. Being a smart ass my whole life made me kind of witty. Since I thought it was my claim to fame, I joined a group that prided itself in being smug and sarcastic. It was my first encounter with a grammar Nazi. Was followed was a battle.

I used to come home and turn on the computer like I was going to a rumble. Hands shaky, my insecurities would scream in my head. I would wonder what she said, thinking how I would whoop her ass. We went on like that for a while. She would use grammar as her weapon. I resorted to street slang and crudeness.

It became evident that while I had learned to stay out of

toxic relationships with men, I gravitated to toxic encounters on social media. After some time, I left the group. Once in a while, I would eavesdrop. Soon enough, I realized the woman lived in Australia or somewhere around. I wondered why I was letting her have so much power.

I guess it comes down to acceptance and fear of rejection. It was the same thought process that led me to men who were not in my best interest. I wanted a big man to feel petite. I wanted a tough guy to feel safe. I guess I wanted good-looking men to feel we were outstanding together. I chose men with issues so they wouldn't judge me. What I got were some lazy ass opportunists and emotional predators.

When a woman talks a lot of shit, she scares away most men. Predators know she is vulnerable, which is why she is acting tough. In other words, by acting street-like or crazy to show you're not 'the one' to mess with, you actually draw men who will exploit your weakness.

I could not understand why so many men and women acted like people they were not. After all, it takes a lot of work to be full of shit. To act like you care about someone just to get hand outs? In reality, they're no more than corny get over artists.

I know I was a piece of work back then. I would spoil people at first and then go spastic on them. I remember reading a quote that went, "If you put a small price on yourself, the world will not raise the price," or something to that effect. I realized it was true.

The last day of school arrived. Not the last day of the semester, but the last day, period. I was graduating with a bachelor's degree in sociology. I spent a lot of time making conversation and meeting new people. It felt like an overload on my nervous system. Every time finals came around, I would get an eye twitch because of stress. As soon finals were over, the twitch would go away.

I was still trying to race onto my next challenge at Hunter Grad School. I had finished in the middle of the summer and hoped it would not be a factor. My GPA sucked. I tried to sell my experiences and make up for it on my application. I had finished in the face of adversity.

I'd been on interferon, living in a shelter for felons that gave me bed bugs, which they said was my fault, because I brought them from my volunteer job. Were they serious? I wouldn't give a fuck if I invited them from an infested midtown movie theater. Fact was they were there, and again, a facility was not taking responsibility. My cries fell on deaf ears.

Then, my luck changed. I got a studio apartment in East Harlem. When I tried to get help for my shoulder and neck, the doctor quipped, "Why should taxpayers pay?" I figured I had to become someone in this game of chess. Being at the bottom of the totem pole was not an option. The only way to beat the streets was to change.

I learned to shut up, for most part, because it was college, not bullpen therapy. My anxiety made it difficult. Besides, several subjects I was studying kicked up emotions.

My last semester consisted of African history and PR studies. It was mind blowing. I found African and Latino studies more intriguing than sociology classes. Subjects I dreaded in the beginning, I grew to learn from and respect. It was still sociology, but instead of terms like Marxism and socialism, it was the raw story.

I had to leave class because of content on a few occasions. When you have been traumatized and victimized, you have empathy. Seeing people victimized made me mad and ashamed of history. There was no way to make sense of what happened in and to Africa. When people like me who don't know shit say stuff like, "Well, they sold their own people out," it's simply a way to dismiss what really happened.

When you learn and understand they were played against each by Colonial powers because Africa was a continent and not a country, it's not a nice feeling. History shows Africa was not united and did not have an army to protect the region in its entirety.

America has a united army that accounts for all states. That does not make us united in other ways such as economical and cultural. My point is, when I say that Africa was not united, I mean they did not have the experience or armory to fight wars.

I learned of what happened in Congo, where Kind Leopold had taken pride in chopping off limbs, even of children, to use as a scare tactic. What kind of savage does that? And they called Africans savages? The king's men made them find rubber from trees so he could get rich. Who the fuck did he think he was? A king, I guess. What a crazy world we lived in, and still do.

Europeans went in and took everything they could get their hands on, including people. They brought them here. When the whites needed the blacks for other reasons, they freed them and played a different power game, sharecropping.

I had a few Irish friends who looked down on blacks. They said the Irish had built themselves up and blacks were just bums. Mind you, the ones telling me this were felons with no education or jobs. I guess we connect ourselves to what we think our heritage is. I thought, as an Irish, I was supposed to get drunk and fight.

I couldn't be the only one out because they are even called a team, the fighting Irish. When I was trying to learn about myself, I learned what happened to Ireland, and I was angry with the English.

It's easy to want to jump on the angry bandwagon and put a face to blame for your inner demons. When you identify with a cause, gang or religion, or try to feel better than another group of people, changing your mind is scary. You feel lost.

I used to fantasize about being a vigilante. It made me want to hurt those who hurt others. To some degree, we all make our own laws, rules and justifications, just like our government.

I remember growing up, being scared at home, hearing some blacks on a corner talking about blue eyed devils. This was around the time when all I heard in school was that Russia was going to nuke us. Talk about Vietnam and its horrors. When even your home doesn't feel safe, it's a scary world.

My friends had grown up on the street and anything that felt like a threat was the enemy. That logic made blacks our main rivals. After all, it was them who over populated our jails. When I saw mass incarceration was designed and orchestrated as an industrial business, and we worked for pennies, I felt we got played.

I worked in welding, where women worked for 26 pennies an hour, making garbage cans for the NYC. Do the math. It's a business. What a fuckin' racket! I realized blacks were the main targets. It made me reassess my outlook and question my immediate reactions. I also felt we were all products of our environments. If a group of people had been traumatized, simply saying sorry was not going to fix it.

The main thing that struck me was nobody wants to say sorry for the past. Not as a person or a color, but as a society. If this country has led a dog eat dog existence and exploited a whole bunch of other countries, stop playing the nice fuckin' guy.

I know life goes on and I don't focus on the past. So what if I also found out what happened in the Caribbean? How the U.S. took over countries' economies and then pulled out, leaving them destitute. It goes on and on.

When Africans or people from other supposed third-world countries come here as a last resort, they are treated like cockroaches in kitchens that need to be squashed. I am not saying any color is good or bad. However, why do all of us take such strong positions when most of us don't know squat?

You can't tell me to go back to Africa because I was born here. Just call me the next best thing. I, like many others, feel success is the best revenge. That way, revenge becomes an afterthought. I realized there was a whole world out there and I wanted to see and learn more. I wanted to go on a vacation because I'd never been on one.

22.
Ground Zero (2016)

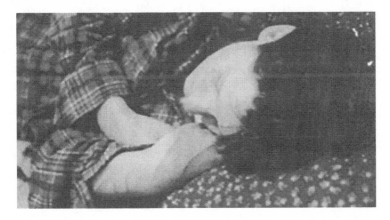

Self- mutilation (1996)

I was not successful getting into grad school on my first attempt. While I felt a little disappointed, it did not slow me down. I told myself I would apply to a few more schools in the following year and that I should not put all my eggs in one basket.

I figured I could use the time to finish this book. I had been working on it for 14 years and could never get around to giving it my all. Besides, I did not know how to focus, edit or promote.

Back in the day, I used to be a little delusional. I swore I should have been on Oprah or in an opera simply because my life sucked. I thought writing a bunch of war stories and about people I hated would get me a bestseller. What I noticed, though, is when you want instant fame and fortune, you're usually disappointed.

Once, I used to walk in the middle of the street and expect cars to stop and drive around. It was only after I got clean and saw behaviors in others that I realized how out of control my ways were. I was finally stable. No drugs for seven years, no cigarettes for seven years and no arrests in seven years.

The building I live in is a low income housing facility where drugs are rampant. The noise and the drug traffic are agitating, to say the least. Nobody knows, better than me that if someone's not ready, there's no sense in preaching.

In my studio apartment, I prioritize anything and everything that can help me heal and enhance my mind and body. I got a back machine, where I hang upside down. I use a treadmill to deal with cholesterol kind of issues as well as to address regular midlife wear and tear. My standup punching bag takes around 50 gallons of water, to keep it stable around the base. Working out helps me deal with anxiety. I do not want to take painkillers. I decided to look for a part-time peer-related job opening and saw an advertisement for a Hepatitis C peer navigator in The Bronx. I sent an email saying I'd just graduated with a bachelor's degree in sociology from Hunter. One of the requirements was applicants should have completed Hepatitis C treatment. When it comes to peer-related jobs, I seem to have all the goodies.

I got a fairly quick response and headed out to The Bronx to see if it was worth a shot. I had worked doing outreach for over two years when I was going to school. Although I met some wonderful people, I was overwhelmed from spreading myself too thin. Imagine going to school full-time, dealing with anxiety attacks, living in a shelter for felons and working part-time on a van. We drove to far ends of the boroughs in all kinds of weather. I eventually quit because a person who worked there.

Since I'd finished school, I was up for a challenge. At my interview, I met a very pretty Hispanic woman who sat me down and asked me questions. She was impressionable and personable. She said the cure for Hepatitis C would be a great way for me to help people. She felt I was the right person.

I told her I was not going to lie and tell people there was a cure because it was not successful at all times. I learned there was new medication and it was not as rough as the treatment I underwent. It offered a 99.7 percent chance of cure as well.

When I told her I was interested she said the job was full-time and asked me what salary was I had in mind. "Huh?" I thought to myself. I didn't know it was full-time. Besides, I never had a salaried job before. I simply didn't know. "I don't know what I'm worth," I said, because it was all-new to me.

She told me I was worth more than I knew, metaphorically, of course, which was fine. I found a job I believed in and someone who cared about people had hired me. When we confirmed the job, she said, "Oh, it's not here, it's at another site." She gave me the address and I froze. I was hoping it was not next to where I lived when my life was a horror story.

Within a year, the whole block where I lived jumped me. I punched someone, feeling I was getting ripped off, and I got hit with sticks. It was a free for all – men, women and kids.

In the past, I had a knife to protect myself, but I ended up stabbing someone. I kicked a cop in the nuts, to get pepper sprayed in return. I got gang raped when working as a call girl. Another incident resulted in a broken nose –, mine. I also got my teeth and head cracked at some point. My boyfriend from that time was dead. His body was missing because no one claimed it in time. You don't call the cops when you're not a value to society, so I never really faced any of it.

That neighborhood scared me. I saw what could happen. It was not paranoia. In the old days, I was out of control. Part of me expected to die a violent death. I had nothing to lose. However, things changed. I was at a stage where I wanted to live.

I figured I could not run away from my past. While I sleep with a light on and have to have a see-through shower curtain so nobody can sneak up on me, I feel I have enough demons to fight. Something told me I had to give changing my life a fighting chance. I went there and started working, loving what I did.

The second week, during lunch, I walked a few blocks and looked up at my old window. The neighborhood had improved but was still rough. It continued being home to a lot of shooting deaths.

I know Jimmy and I had a crazy relationship, unlike him, I was able to turn my life around. He lost his family by the age of 13 and never had a chance, at least, not a good one. I am still trying to locate his body. He remains in an unmarked grave somewhere and that is not what I want for him. He was only 31 years old.

We might not have had the coping skills to have a healthy relationship. I was just as lost as him, and more reckless.

I still work as a Hepatitis C peer navigator and plan to keep doing it for some time. I know the damage that drugs do to the family cycle and self-worth of every individual involved. I tell people in my group they don't have to accept labels society puts on them. I ask them to stop fighting over TVs and chairs, and fight for a better life instead, because everyone deserves a chance. I love my job because I am telling and helping people learn to invest in themselves and the treatment for Hepatitis -C is available and much improved. Less time & far fewer side effects. I see most of the icons politicians, celebrities and the likes – are not very impressive. I guess being full of shit is part of their job descriptions. Therefore, I like my job title, which says 'navigator.' The word is instrumental in the transitioning of a sub-cultural being with a pattern of self-sabotage into one who can integrate into society in a productive, positive and empowered way.

Yesterday, I went to Columbia University with an R.S.V.P, to see what they had on offer for graduate school. I am mentioning this because not so long ago, around four years back, I used to cut through their campus – it was easier than walking an extra five blocks to go around.

There were gated security stations at both ends. When I walked through, I felt rather uncomfortable, like I didn't belong there. I felt security was going to ask me why I was there. From working on the street as a prostitute, I gained some degree of self-loathing. I felt ugly when it came to presentation.

I feel the country, and probably the world, is all about presentation and delivery. When you've not made peace with yourself, you carry that pain and lack of self-worth. I might walk with bravado and be the queen of sarcasm with my witty responses, but that's just a mask.

While I have major work to do on myself, getting an invitation from a school I used to be afraid of walking though felt wonderful.

If I was walking through a hostile street, I would, at times, pretend it wasn't real and that it was a painting instead. In the new scenario, I was not in danger but still felt uncomfortable. I guess I felt I didn't belong.

After some time, I realized nobody was going to arrest me for trespassing. I was like everyone else, just as human.

Now, I walk into Columbia as a possible future student. I might not get in and I might not be able to afford it, but the feeling of inferiority is fading away fast.

Final Thoughts

I watched, studied and judged the world through a critical eye
judging others as I felt I had been judged
You can study all the wrongs in the world to your heart's content
in truth, your heart remains far from content
It feels cold and empty
Like a war staged in your soul, the bodies still there
Rotting and waiting for recognition
Bitterness grows like cancer
Labeled by society, a criminal
If I'm the bad guy, why does the world seem so scary?

I realize there are bigger battles to fight and I'm entitled to more than basic needs and day-to-day living with no sense of security. Being a rebel was fun, for a while. When I was intoxicated, it was like doing the dance of self-sabotage.

Now, I know I'm entitled to living, loving and finding peace with others and myself. I know everything is not a competition. I see my peers fighting over crumbs such as chairs and TV's, jumping in front of each other to be first in lines, and being hateful and putting each other down to feel superior   because they feel like failures in the real world. I see myself in my peers and my clients.

I am awake now. Although far from perfect, I help others heal instead of hurting them. It nourishes my soul. You are, after all, the energy you emit.

My bitterness started melting away because I could see much further. Although learning about the world was bittersweet, it felt like a wave of relief. I realized there was so much more to life than being mad or judgmental.

We debate and state what we hear even when our sources are tainted. Why preach hate when it has been passed down to you like the flu, a virus?

I do not claim or disclaim any religion. How can I, when I have never been there or met a God? My higher power is a belief in positive energy. I have always acknowledged evil but never gave good a chance. Even if it's all a farce, whatever we believe in, as long as it helps us cope and coexist with others, it should be alright.

Learning about the history and struggles of other cultures showed me the problem is a much bigger than jail. We are symptoms of a much bigger core problem. Whatever you previously thought, it's time you re-think. We are all works in progress.

If you think the same way you did 20 years ago, you need to get out more often. Part of being comfortable with others in society is finding comfort in your own skin and learning about others in a non-hostile environment.

One of my favorite songs was, and is, Everlast's "What it's like." How can we try to judge others when we have not walked a mile in their shoes? Although I'm trying to change the seeds I plant in my thought garden, I still relate to songs that bring raw logical music with a good beat.

It's time to help others find clarity, give them hope
Show your peers the future is brighter than violence and jails
It's not all about out-twerking your neighbor and being objectified
Show the youth in fear the future has a comfort zone and a safe place
Provided they believe
Navigate and learn about the system that oppresses you
build a real foundation
Don't be fooled by the seduction of immediate gratification

After the Turnaround

And Finally, My Woman Cave!

Everyone needs a foundation
A safe place to go and plan the rest of their life

Made in the USA
Lexington, KY
11 February 2017